VEGAN SuperFood

First Edition: 2023

Published by Taste of Vegan

Printed in USA

The recipes, techniques, and tips in this cookbook are intended for personal use only. The author and publisher are not responsible for any adverse effects or consequences resulting from the use of the recipes or suggestions in this book.

Library of Congress Cataloging-in-Publication Data:

First edition.
Includes index.

Manufactured in USA

Introduction

Ladies and gentlemen, fellow culinary adventurers, and seekers of nourishing delights, I extend to you a heartfelt welcome to the world of "Vegan Superfood." Within these pages, we embark on a journey that celebrates the essence of plant-based superfoods, igniting your taste buds and nurturing your well-being.

This cookbook is a labor of love, a testament to the boundless potential of plant-based eating. In a world filled with processed foods and dietary confusion, the focus here is clear: to harness the vibrant energy and exceptional nutrition that superfoods offer. It's about embracing a diet that not only satisfies your palate but also nourishes your body from the inside out.

As the author, my inspiration for creating this cookbook stems from a deep-rooted belief in the power of food as medicine. I've witnessed firsthand the transformative effects of incorporating superfoods into one's daily diet. The energy surge, the clarity of mind, and the vitality that ensue are nothing short of remarkable. I'm driven by a desire to share these experiences with you, to demystify the world of superfoods, and to show that they can be both accessible and delicious.

Within the pages of "Vegan Superfood," you can expect to find a tantalizing array of recipes that showcase the versatility of plant-based superfoods. From vibrant smoothie bowls bursting with antioxidants to hearty grain bowls brimming with nutrients, each dish is a celebration of natural ingredients that nourish and invigorate. The recipes are accompanied by stunning pictures that capture the vibrant colors and textures of these superfood creations, inspiring you to embark on your own culinary adventures.

Throughout this journey, we'll explore the tastes and textures of superfoods like kale, quinoa, chia seeds, and more. You'll discover how to seamlessly incorporate these nutritional powerhouses into your daily meals, from breakfast to dinner and everything in between.

So, as you turn the pages of "Vegan Superfood," prepare to be inspired, educated, and empowered. Whether you're a seasoned vegan or just beginning to explore the world of plant-based eating, this cookbook is your passport to a healthier, more vibrant you. Welcome to a world where food is not just sustenance but a source of vitality, where superfoods take center stage, and where every bite is a step towards a healthier, happier you.

Acai Berry
Smoothie Bowl
See page, 6

Cooking Philosophy or Approach

Welcome to the vibrant world of "Vegan Superfood," where we embark on a culinary journey that celebrates the power and deliciousness of plant-based superfoods. This cookbook isn't just about recipes; it's about a philosophy, an approach to cooking that embraces nature's gifts and transforms them into delightful, nourishing meals.

Cooking Philosophy and Approach:

My approach to cooking is rooted in simplicity, health, and the incredible bounty of nature. I believe that food should not only be a source of sustenance but also a celebration of life. It's about fueling our bodies with the best ingredients while indulging our taste buds in a symphony of flavors.

At the heart of this cookbook is a deep appreciation for the incredible superfoods that Mother Earth provides us. These nutrient-dense, plant-based powerhouses are the cornerstone of our recipes. They're not just ingredients; they're the building blocks of a healthier, more vibrant life.

Techniques and Ingredients:

Throughout these pages, you'll find recipes that showcase the beauty and versatility of superfoods. From kale and quinoa to chia seeds and spirulina, each ingredient is carefully chosen for its health benefits and culinary potential.

Our approach to cooking these superfoods is all about balance. We embrace techniques like roasting, sautéing, and blending to bring out their natural flavors and maximize their nutritional value. But we also recognize the importance of simplicity. Sometimes, the best way to enjoy a superfood is in its raw, unadulterated form.

You'll also notice that our recipes draw inspiration from various culinary traditions. We believe in the global diversity of flavors and ingredients, and we bring them together harmoniously in our dishes. Whether it's the creaminess of an avocado-based sauce or the bold spices of a turmeric-infused curry, we aim to delight your taste buds while nourishing your body.

In "Vegan Superfood," you'll find a blend of innovative recipes and classic favorites, all with one common thread: the inclusion of superfoods that elevate the nutritional profile of each dish. Our goal is to make superfood eating accessible and enjoyable, whether you're a seasoned plant-based enthusiast or just starting your journey toward a healthier, more vibrant you.

So, as you delve into these recipes, I encourage you to embrace the philosophy of "Vegan Superfood." Let's celebrate the incredible potential of plant-based superfoods together, one delicious bite at a time.

Thai-Inspired
Vegan Noodle Salad
See page, 19

Tips for Successful Cooking

Ah, my fellow culinary explorers, as we delve into the realm of "Vegan Superfood," I must first extend my warmest welcome to you all. Here, we embark on a journey of nourishment and vitality, exploring the wonders of plant-based superfoods that fuel both body and soul.

But before we immerse ourselves in the world of superfood delights, let's take a moment to discuss the essential tools that will be our trusty companions on this culinary adventure. These are the tips and techniques that will not only help us master the recipes within this cookbook but will also elevate our cooking skills to new heights.

General Cooking Tips:

1. Preparation is Key: Just as a seasoned traveler plans their journey meticulously, a skilled cook must prepare in advance. Read through the recipe thoroughly before starting to ensure you have all the ingredients and equipment required.

2. Organization is Vital: Create a workspace that is efficient and organized. Mis en place, a French term for "everything in its place," should be your mantra. Arrange all your ingredients and utensils within easy reach.

3. Taste as You Go: Seasoning is an art form, and your palate is your best guide. Taste your dishes as you cook, adjusting seasonings gradually to achieve the perfect balance of flavors.

4. Patience is a Virtue: Superfoods often require gentle handling. Be patient with your cooking processes, whether it's slow-roasting, simmering, or marinating. The rewards are well worth the time invested.

5. Experiment and Adapt: Don't be afraid to add your personal touch to the recipes. Experiment with different superfoods and herbs to discover your own unique creations.

Ingredient Selection:

1. Fresh is Best: Whenever possible, choose fresh, organic superfoods. Their vibrant colors and flavors are a testament to their nutritional potency.

2. Mindful Substitutions: If you need to make substitutions, do so with consideration. Select ingredients that complement the dish's overall flavor profile and nutritional value.

3. Seasonal Sensibility: Embrace seasonal superfoods. Not only are they more affordable, but they also connect you to the rhythms of nature.

Preparation and Cooking Methods:

1. Gentle Heat: Superfoods often benefit from gentle cooking methods like steaming, sautéing, or blanching to preserve their nutrients and flavors.

2. Embrace Rawness: Some superfoods are best enjoyed in their raw state to maximize their health benefits. Experiment with salads, smoothies, and raw desserts to harness their full potential.

3. Blending and Grinding: Invest in a high-quality blender and grinder. These appliances are essential for creating smooth, creamy textures and extracting maximum nutrition from superfoods.

Now, my friends, armed with these essential cooking tips, ingredient selection advice, and preparation techniques, you are well-prepared to embark on your culinary journey through "Vegan Superfood." The world of plant-based superfoods awaits, promising not only delicious flavors but also vibrant health.

As we delve deeper into this superfood odyssey, remember to embrace your creativity, savor the process, and relish the nourishment that these ingredients offer. The kitchen is your canvas, and the superfoods, your palette. Bon appétit!

Vegan Breakfast Tacos
See page, 39

Kitchen Essentials

Welcome, fellow culinary explorers, to the world of "Vegan Superfood"! As we embark on this plant-based journey through the realm of superfoods, I want to provide you with the essential tools and knowledge to conquer your kitchen like a seasoned chef. In the spirit of adventure and nourishment, let's delve into our kitchen essentials.

Kitchen Essentials:

1. High-Speed Blender: Your trusty sidekick for whipping up smoothies, soups, and sauces with the power to blend superfoods into creamy perfection.

2. Food Processor: A multitasking marvel for chopping, slicing, and dicing superfood ingredients to elevate your dishes.

3. Quality Knives: A set of sharp, high-quality knives is your gateway to precision and efficiency in the kitchen.

4. Cutting Board: A durable and spacious cutting board provides a stable surface for all your chopping endeavors.

5. Cast Iron Skillet: The seasoned hero of the stovetop, perfect for searing and cooking superfood-packed meals.

6. Non-Stick Pan: Ideal for sautéing without excessive oil, ensuring your superfood dishes are both healthy and delicious.

7. Baking Sheets: Essential for roasting superfood-laden vegetables to perfection.

8. Steamer Basket: A steamer basket lets you preserve the nutrients and vibrant colors of superfoods while keeping them tender.

9. Microplane Grater/Zester: For adding citrus zest and finely grating superfood ingredients with ease.

10. Measuring Cups and Spoons: Precision in measurements is key when working with superfoods.

Tips on Using These Tools Effectively:

1. Blender Mastery: When using a high-speed blender, start at low speed and gradually increase to prevent splattering. Blend until smooth for the creamiest results.

2. Food Processor Finesse: Ensure your food processor is properly assembled before use. For even chopping, pulse rather than running continuously.

3. Knife Skills: Keep your knives sharp; a dull knife is more dangerous than a sharp one. Learn proper knife techniques to slice, dice, and chop superfoods effortlessly.

4. Care for Your Cast Iron: Season your cast iron skillet regularly to maintain its non-stick surface. Avoid using soap and opt for a gentle scrub to clean it.

5. Balanced Sautéing: Use a minimal amount of oil when sautéing. Start with onions and garlic to infuse flavor into your superfood dishes.

6. Roasting Bliss: Preheat your baking sheets before adding vegetables to ensure even cooking. Don't overcrowd the pan to prevent steaming instead of roasting.

7. Steaming Superfoods: Use a steamer basket over boiling water to preserve the texture and nutritional value of your superfood ingredients.

8. Zest with Gusto: When using a microplane grater, hold it at a slight angle and zest only the colored part of citrus fruits to avoid the bitter pith.

9. Precision in Measurements: Measure dry and liquid ingredients accurately for consistent results when working with superfoods.

Armed with these kitchen essentials and expert tips, you're well-equipped to embark on your superfood journey. The world of plant-based, nutrient-packed delights awaits you, and I can't wait to see what incredible creations you'll whip up in your kitchen. So, my fellow culinary adventurers, don your aprons, sharpen your knives, and let the superfood feast begin!

Flavor Pairing Suggestions

Ah, my fellow culinary adventurers, as we reach the heart of "Vegan Superfood," our gastronomic journey takes a delightful turn. We've immersed ourselves in the vibrant world of plant-based superfoods, exploring the bountiful offerings of nature that nourish both body and soul.

But before we delve further into the realm of flavor pairings, allow me to express my deepest appreciation for your unwavering curiosity and dedication. It's the intrepid spirit of food lovers like you that keeps the culinary fire burning bright.

Now, let's talk about something that's like the secret ingredient in the recipe of culinary creativity: flavor pairing. It's where the magic happens, where ingredients harmonize, and where taste buds dance in joyful union.

In the world of plant-based superfoods, the possibilities are as vast as the Amazon rainforest. Consider pairing the earthy richness of kale with the zesty tang of lemon, or the creamy decadence of avocado with the nutty crunch of almonds. The sweetness of ripe berries might find its perfect match in the dark allure of cacao nibs. These are just a few sparks to ignite your culinary imagination.

In this section, we offer you a treasure trove of flavor pairing suggestions. Think of them as your passport to culinary exploration. They're ideas, but also invitations to experiment, create, and discover your own taste symphonies.

Remember, the world of plant-based superfoods is a lush garden of possibilities. It's where textures, colors, and flavors converge to create unforgettable dining experiences. So, don your apron, sharpen your knives, and let your palate be your guide.

As we journey deeper into the realm of Vegan Superfood, may your culinary creations be as vibrant and nourishing as the superfoods themselves. And as always, remember that food is a celebration of life, a symphony of flavors, and a testament to the beauty of the natural world.

Table of contents

Chapter 1
Energizing Breakfasts

2
servings

350
calories

15
minutes

Quinoa Breakfast Bowl

Ingredients:

- 1 cup cooked quinoa
- 1/2 cup almond milk
- 1/2 cup fresh berries
- 1/4 cup chopped nuts
- 1 tbsp honey
- A pinch of cinnamon

Rise and shine with this protein-packed delight. A blend of quinoa, fresh fruits, and nuts - a morning ritual that started in the Andes and found its way to our hearts.

Directions

1. Cook quinoa according to package instructions.
2. In a bowl, mix quinoa, almond milk, and honey.
3. Top with berries, nuts, and a pinch of cinnamon.
4. Serve with love and enjoy!

Substitutions

None

4
servings

280
calories

25
minutes

Sweet Potato and Chickpea Breakfast Hash

A hearty and healthy breakfast with a twist. Sweet potatoes and chickpeas dance together in perfect harmony.

Ingredients:

- 2 sweet potatoes, diced
- 1 can chickpeas, drained
- 1 onion, chopped
- 2 cloves garlic, minced
- 1 tsp paprika
- Salt and pepper to taste

Directions

1. Heat oil in a skillet, add onions and garlic, sauté until fragrant.
2. Add sweet potatoes, cook until golden.
3. Add chickpeas, paprika, salt, and pepper. Cook until everything is crispy.
4. Serve hot and enjoy!

Substitutions

None

 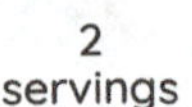  

2
servings

320
calories

20
minutes

Avocado and Kale Breakfast Burrito

An avocado lover's dream! Creamy avo and nutrient-rich kale wrapped in a tortilla for a morning fiesta.

Ingredients:

- 2 whole wheat tortillas
- 1 avocado, mashed
- 1 cup kale, chopped
- 1/2 cup black beans, cooked
- 1/4 cup diced tomatoes
- Hot sauce (optional)

Directions

1. Lay out tortillas and spread mashed avocado.
2. Top with kale, black beans, and tomatoes.
3. Add hot sauce if you like a kick!
4. Roll up, slice in half, and savor the goodness.

Substitutions

Hot sauce for heat

2
servings

220
calories

10
minutes

Vegan Chia Seed Pudding

Ingredients:

- 1/4 cup chia seeds
- 1 cup almond milk
- 1 tbsp maple syrup
- 1/2 tsp vanilla extract
- Fresh fruit for topping

A velvety delight for your morning cravings. Chia seeds soaked in almond milk, sweetened to perfection.

Directions

1. In a jar, mix chia seeds, almond milk, maple syrup, and vanilla.
2. Stir well and refrigerate for at least 2 hours or overnight.
3. Top with fresh fruit and indulge in a guilt-free treat.

Substitutions

None

2 servings	290 calories	10 minutes

Acai Berry Smoothie Bowl

Ingredients:

- 2 packs frozen acai puree
- 1/2 cup almond milk
- 1/2 cup frozen mixed berries
- 1 banana
- Toppings: granola, coconut, and more berries

Substitutions

Toppings as desired

Dive into the vibrant world of acai berries and feel the tropical vibes with every spoonful.

Directions

1. Blend acai, almond milk, frozen berries, and banana until smooth.
2. Pour into a bowl and top with your favorite toppings.
3. Savor the taste of the Amazon rainforest right at your breakfast table.

2
servings

250
calories

5
minutes

Vegan Overnight Oats

Ingredients:

- 1 cup rolled oats
- 1 1/2 cups almond milk
- 2 tbsp maple syrup
- 1/2 tsp cinnamon
- Fresh fruit for topping

Prepare breakfast the night before and wake up to a nutritious delight. Oats, almond milk, and a touch of magic.

Directions

1. Mix oats, almond milk, maple syrup, and cinnamon in a jar.
2. Refrigerate overnight.
3. Top with fresh fruit in the morning and savor your time-saving masterpiece.

Substitutions

None

4
servings

180
calories

15
minutes

Tofu Scramble with Spinach and Mushrooms

Ingredients:

- 1 block firm tofu, crumbled
- 1 cup spinach
- 1 cup mushrooms, sliced
- 1/2 onion, chopped
- 1 tsp turmeric
- Salt and pepper to taste

Substitutions

None

For the savory lovers! Tofu, spinach, and mushrooms unite in a protein-packed morning dance.

Directions

1. Heat oil in a pan, sauté onions and mushrooms until tender.
2. Add tofu, turmeric, salt, and pepper, cook until heated through.
3. Stir in spinach until wilted.
4. Serve hot, and experience the magic of tofu scramble.

4
servings

320
calories

20
minutes

Peanut Butter Banana Protein Pancakes

Ingredients:

- 1 cup whole wheat flour
- 1 scoop protein powder
- 1 ripe banana, mashed
- 2 tbsp peanut butter
- 1 tsp baking powder
- 1 cup almond milk

Substitutions

None

Fluffy and protein-packed pancakes to kickstart your day. Peanut butter and bananas in every bite.

Directions

1. In a bowl, mix flour, protein powder, banana, peanut butter, and baking powder.
2. Add almond milk to achieve desired consistency.
3. Cook on a hot griddle until golden brown.
4. Stack 'em up and dig in!

2 servings · **280 calories** · **15 minutes**

Blueberry Almond Breakfast Quinoa

Quinoa takes a sweet turn with blueberries and almonds. A delightful twist on a classic grain.

Ingredients:

- 1 cup cooked quinoa
- 1/2 cup almond milk
- 1/2 cup fresh blueberries
- 2 tbsp sliced almonds
- 1 tbsp honey
- A pinch of nutmeg

Directions

1. Combine quinoa, almond milk, blueberries, and almonds in a bowl.
2. Drizzle with honey and sprinkle with nutmeg.
3. Dive into this sweet, nutty paradise.

Substitutions

None

 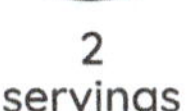  

2
servings

180
calories

10
minutes

Turmeric Ginger Breakfast Smoothie

Ingredients:

- 1 cup orange juice
- 1/2 cup almond milk
- 1 banana
- 1 tsp turmeric
- 1/2 tsp ginger
- 1 tbsp honey (optional)

Wake up your senses with this zesty smoothie. Turmeric, ginger, and citrus for a refreshing start.

Directions

1. Blend orange juice, almond milk, banana, turmeric, and ginger until smooth.
2. Add honey if desired for sweetness.
3. Sip slowly and let the flavors awaken your day.

Substitutions

Honey for sweetness

Chapter 2
Satisfying Lunches

2
servings

380
calories

20
minutes

Vegan Buddha Bowl

A harmonious blend of grains, greens, and wholesome goodness.

Ingredients:

- 1 cup cooked quinoa
- 1 cup chickpeas, roasted
- 2 cups mixed greens
- 1 cup roasted sweet potatoes
- 1/2 avocado, sliced
- Tahini dressing: 2 tbsp tahini, 2 tbsp lemon juice, 1 clove garlic, minced, water to thin

Directions

1. Prepare quinoa according to package instructions.
2. Roast chickpeas and sweet potatoes until crispy.
3. In a bowl, layer quinoa, greens, chickpeas, sweet potatoes, and avocado.
4. Drizzle with tahini dressing.
5. Devour the harmony!

Substitutions

None

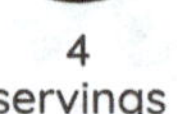

4
servings

320
calories

15
minutes

Mediterranean Quinoa Salad

Ingredients:

- 1 cup quinoa, cooked
- 1 cup cucumber, diced
- 1 cup cherry tomatoes, halved
- 1/2 cup Kalamata olives, pitted
- 1/4 cup red onion, finely chopped
- 1/4 cup fresh parsley, chopped
- Lemon vinaigrette: 2 tbsp olive oil, 2 tbsp lemon juice, 1 tsp dried oregano

Transport your taste buds to the shores of the Mediterranean.

Directions

1. In a large bowl, combine quinoa, cucumber, tomatoes, olives, onion, and parsley.
2. Whisk together the lemon vinaigrette ingredients and drizzle over the salad.
3. Toss gently to coat.
4. Serve and savor the Mediterranean flavors.

Substitutions

None

4
servings

250
calories

30
minutes

Vegan Lentil Soup

A hearty bowl of comfort, packed with protein and rich flavors.

Ingredients:

- 1 cup green lentils, rinsed
- 1 onion, chopped
- 2 carrots, diced
- 2 celery stalks, chopped
- 3 cloves garlic, minced
- 1 tsp cumin
- 1 tsp paprika
- 6 cups vegetable broth
- Salt and pepper to taste

Directions

1. In a large pot, sauté onions, carrots, celery, and garlic until softened.
2. Add lentils, cumin, and paprika; cook for a few minutes.
3. Pour in vegetable broth and bring to a boil.
4. Simmer until lentils are tender.
5. Season with salt and pepper.
6. Enjoy the warmth and nourishment.

Substitutions

None

2
servings

340
calories

25
minutes

Spicy Vegan Ramen

Ingredients:

- 2 packs ramen noodles (discard seasoning packets)
- 4 cups vegetable broth
- 1 block tofu, cubed
- 1 cup sliced mushrooms
- 2 cups bok choy, chopped
- 2 tbsp soy sauce
- 1 tsp sriracha (adjust to taste)

Substitutions

Adjust sriracha for spice level

Kick up your lunch with this fiery bowl of vegan ramen.

Directions

1. Cook ramen noodles according to package instructions, drain, and set aside.
2. In a pot, bring vegetable broth to a simmer.
3. Add tofu, mushrooms, bok choy, soy sauce, and sriracha.
4. Simmer until veggies are tender.
5. Serve ramen over cooked noodles.
6. Slurp away!

2
servings

280
calories

20
minutes

Roasted Veggie and Hummus Wrap

A quick and tasty wrap loaded with roasted veggies and creamy hummus.

Ingredients:

- 2 whole wheat tortillas
- 1 cup mixed roasted veggies (bell peppers, zucchini, eggplant, etc.)
- 1/2 cup hummus
- Fresh greens for filling

Directions

1. Lay out tortillas and spread hummus evenly.
2. Add a generous portion of roasted veggies.
3. Top with fresh greens.
4. Roll up the wraps and cut in half.
5. Delight in the flavors and textures.

Substitutions

None

2
servings

290
calories

15
minutes

Vegan Chickpea Salad Sandwich

A protein-packed, satisfying sandwich that's perfect for lunch.

Ingredients:

- 1 can chickpeas, drained and mashed
- 1/4 cup vegan mayo
- 1/4 cup diced celery
- 2 tbsp red onion, finely chopped
- 1 tsp Dijon mustard
- Salt and pepper to taste
- Lettuce and whole wheat bread for the sandwich

Directions

1. In a bowl, mix mashed chickpeas, vegan mayo, celery, red onion, and Dijon mustard.
2. Season with salt and pepper.
3. Assemble sandwiches with chickpea salad and lettuce.
4. Bite into the goodness and enjoy!

Substitutions

None

4
servings

340
calories

20
minutes

Thai-Inspired Vegan Noodle Salad

Ingredients:

- 8 oz rice noodles, cooked
- 1 cup mixed bell peppers, thinly sliced
- 1 cup shredded carrots
- 1/2 cucumber, thinly sliced
- 1/4 cup fresh cilantro, chopped
- Peanut dressing: 2 tbsp peanut butter, 2 tbsp soy sauce, 1 tbsp rice vinegar, 1 tbsp maple syrup

A vibrant noodle salad bursting with Thai-inspired flavors.

Directions

1. In a large bowl, combine cooked rice noodles, bell peppers, carrots, cucumber, and cilantro.
2. Whisk together the peanut dressing ingredients and drizzle over the salad.
3. Toss to coat.
4. Dive into the vibrant Thai flavors.

Substitutions

None

2
servings

320
calories

25
minutes

Vegan Sweet Potato and Black Bean Quesadilla

Ingredients:

- 2 whole wheat tortillas
- 1 cup sweet potatoes, diced and roasted
- 1 cup black beans, cooked
- 1/2 cup corn kernels
- 1/2 cup vegan cheese, shredded
- Salsa for dipping

Substitutions

None

A delightful quesadilla stuffed with sweet potatoes and black beans.

Directions

1. Lay out tortillas and sprinkle vegan cheese on one half of each tortilla.
2. Layer with roasted sweet potatoes, black beans, and corn.
3. Fold tortillas in half.
4. Heat a skillet, cook quesadillas until cheese melts and tortillas are golden.
5. Serve with salsa.
6. Enjoy the cheesy goodness.

2
servings

220
calories

15
minutes

Vegan Caesar Salad

A classic Caesar salad made vegan and oh-so-creamy.

Ingredients:

- 1 head romaine lettuce, chopped
- Croutons (store-bought or homemade)
- Vegan Caesar dressing: 1/4 cup vegan mayo, 1 tbsp lemon juice, 1 clove garlic, minced, 1 tsp Dijon mustard, salt and pepper to taste

Directions

1. In a large bowl, toss chopped romaine lettuce with croutons.
2. Whisk together the vegan Caesar dressing ingredients and drizzle over the salad.
3. Toss until well-coated.
4. Dive into the creamy, crunchy Caesar goodness.

Substitutions

None

4 servings

290 calories

30 minutes

Vegan Black-Eyed Pea Stew

A hearty stew filled with black-eyed peas and savory goodness.

Ingredients:

- 2 cups cooked black-eyed peas
- 1 onion, chopped
- 2 cloves garlic, minced
- 2 carrots, diced
- 2 celery stalks, chopped
- 1 can diced tomatoes
- 4 cups vegetable broth
- 1 tsp smoked paprika
- Salt and pepper to taste

Directions

1. In a large pot, sauté onions, garlic, carrots, and celery until softened.
2. Add black-eyed peas, diced tomatoes, vegetable broth, and smoked paprika.
3. Simmer until flavors meld.
4. Season with salt and pepper.
5. Savor the heartiness of this stew.

Substitutions

None

Chapter 3
Hearty Dinners

4
servings

360
calories

45
minutes

Vegan Lentil Meatballs with Spaghetti

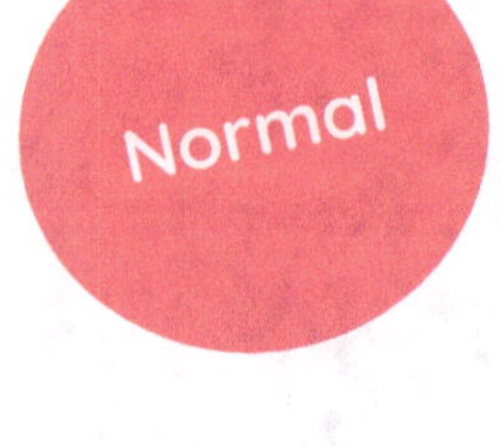

A hearty twist on a classic Italian favorite, perfect for a comforting dinner.

Ingredients:

- 1 cup red lentils, cooked
- 1/2 cup breadcrumbs
- 1/4 cup ground flaxseed
- 1/4 cup chopped onion
- 2 cloves garlic, minced
- 2 tsp Italian seasoning
- Salt and pepper to taste
- Spaghetti and marinara sauce

Directions

1. In a bowl, combine cooked lentils, breadcrumbs, flaxseed, onion, garlic, Italian seasoning, salt, and pepper.
2. Roll mixture into meatballs.
3. Bake at 375°F (190°C) for 20-25 minutes, or until firm.
4. Serve over cooked spaghetti with marinara sauce.
5. Savor the vegan Italian goodness!

Substitutions

None

4
servings

280
calories

30
minutes

Vegan Thai Red Curry

Ingredients:

- 1 can coconut milk
- 2 tbsp red curry paste
- 1 cup mixed vegetables (bell peppers, broccoli, carrots, etc.)
- 1 cup tofu, cubed
- 1 tbsp soy sauce
- 1 tbsp brown sugar
- Fresh basil leaves for garnish

Substitutions

None

Take your taste buds on a journey to Thailand with this fragrant red curry.

Directions

1. In a pan, heat coconut milk and red curry paste until fragrant.
2. Add mixed vegetables, tofu, soy sauce, and brown sugar.
3. Simmer until veggies are tender.
4. Serve over rice or noodles, garnished with fresh basil.
5. Enjoy the aromatic flavors of Thailand.

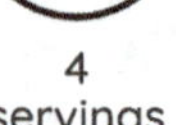

4
servings

320
calories

30
minutes

Vegan Mushroom Stroganoff

Ingredients:

- 8 oz fettuccine or pasta of your choice
- 2 cups sliced mushrooms
- 1 onion, chopped
- 2 cloves garlic, minced
- 1 cup vegetable broth
- 1 cup cashew cream (blend 1 cup soaked cashews with water)
- 2 tbsp nutritional yeast
- Salt and pepper to taste

Substitutions

None

Creamy and indulgent, this mushroom stroganoff is a vegan comfort food dream.

Directions

1. Cook pasta according to package instructions, drain, and set aside.
2. In a skillet, sauté mushrooms, onion, and garlic until tender.
3. Add vegetable broth, cashew cream, nutritional yeast, salt, and pepper.
4. Simmer until the sauce thickens.
5. Serve over cooked pasta.
6. Relish in the creamy goodness.

4
servings

280
calories

30
minutes

Vegan BBQ Pulled Jackfruit Sandwich

A barbecue favorite gone vegan, with tender jackfruit and smoky flavors.

Ingredients:

- 2 cans young green jackfruit in water, drained and shredded
- 1 cup barbecue sauce
- 4 whole wheat buns
- Coleslaw (optional)

Directions

1. In a pan, sauté shredded jackfruit until it begins to brown.
2. Add barbecue sauce and simmer until jackfruit is coated.
3. Toast buns.
4. Assemble sandwiches with pulled jackfruit and coleslaw if desired.
5. Sink your teeth into the barbecue bliss.

Substitutions

Coleslaw if desired

4
servings

320
calories

40
minutes

Vegan Butternut Squash Risotto

Ingredients:

- 1 1/2 cups Arborio rice
- 4 cups vegetable broth
- 2 cups butternut squash, diced and roasted
- 1 onion, chopped
- 2 cloves garlic, minced
- 1/2 cup white wine
- 2 tbsp nutritional yeast
- Salt and pepper to taste

Substitutions

None

Creamy and comforting, this butternut squash risotto is a true autumn delight.

Directions

1. In a large pan, sauté onion and garlic until translucent.
2. Add Arborio rice and cook for a few minutes.
3. Pour in white wine and stir until absorbed.
4. Gradually add vegetable broth, stirring continuously until rice is creamy.
5. Fold in roasted butternut squash, nutritional yeast, salt, and pepper.
6. Savor the rich and creamy flavors.

4
servings

340
calories

35
minutes

Vegan Chickpea Tikka Masala

Ingredients:

- 2 cans chickpeas, drained
- 1 onion, chopped
- 2 cloves garlic, minced
- 1 can diced tomatoes
- 1/2 cup coconut milk
- 2 tbsp tomato paste
- 2 tbsp tikka masala spice blend
- Salt and pepper to taste

A fragrant and spicy chickpea tikka masala that's a vegan favorite.

Directions

1. In a pan, sauté onions and garlic until soft.
2. Add chickpeas, diced tomatoes, coconut milk, tomato paste, tikka masala spice blend, salt, and pepper.
3. Simmer until flavors meld and sauce thickens.
4. Serve over rice, garnish with cilantro.
5. Enjoy the spicy goodness.

Substitutions

None

 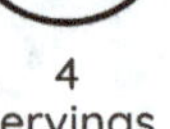  

4
servings

260
calories

45
minutes

Vegan Eggplant Parmesan

Ingredients:

- 2 eggplants, sliced into rounds
- 1 cup breadcrumbs
- 1/4 cup nutritional yeast
- 2 cups marinara sauce
- 1 cup vegan mozzarella cheese
- Fresh basil leaves for garnish

Substitutions

None

Layers of crispy eggplant and marinara sauce,
topped with vegan cheese.

Directions

1. Preheat oven to 375°F (190°C).
2. In a bowl, combine breadcrumbs and nutritional yeast.
3. Dip eggplant slices into the breadcrumb mixture, coating evenly.
4. Arrange on a baking sheet and bake until crispy.
5. In a baking dish, layer marinara sauce, baked eggplant slices, and vegan mozzarella cheese.
6. Bake until cheese is bubbly and golden.
7. Garnish with fresh basil and savor the layers of flavor.

4
servings

320
calories

30
minutes

Vegan Sweet Potato and Chickpea Curry

Ingredients:

- 2 sweet potatoes, diced
- 2 cans chickpeas, drained
- 1 onion, chopped
- 2 cloves garlic, minced
- 2 cups coconut milk
- 2 tbsp curry powder
- Salt and pepper to taste

A warm and comforting curry filled with sweet potatoes and chickpeas.

Directions

1. In a pot, sauté onion and garlic until fragrant.
2. Add diced sweet potatoes, chickpeas, coconut milk, curry powder, salt, and pepper.
3. Simmer until sweet potatoes are tender.
4. Serve over rice or quinoa.
5. Warm up with this hearty curry.

Substitutions

None

4
servings

280
calories

40
minutes

Vegan Quinoa Stuffed Bell Peppers

Bell peppers stuffed with a protein-packed quinoa and veggie mixture.

Ingredients:

- 4 bell peppers, halved and seeds removed
- 1 cup quinoa, cooked
- 1 can black beans, drained
- 1 cup corn kernels
- 1 cup diced tomatoes
- 1/2 cup diced red onion
- 1 tsp chili powder
- Salt and pepper to taste

Directions

1. Preheat oven to 375°F (190°C).
2. In a bowl, mix cooked quinoa, black beans, corn, diced tomatoes, red onion, chili powder, salt, and pepper.
3. Fill bell pepper halves with the quinoa mixture.
4. Bake until peppers are tender.
5. Savor the stuffed pepper goodness.

Substitutions

None

4
servings

260
calories

30
minutes

Vegan Teriyaki Tofu Stir-Fry

Ingredients:

- 1 block firm tofu, cubed
- 1 cup broccoli florets
- 1 bell pepper, sliced
- 1 carrot, thinly sliced
- 2 cloves garlic, minced
- 1/4 cup teriyaki sauce
- Cooked rice for serving

Substitutions

None

A flavorful and saucy tofu stir-fry that's quick to make and packed with umami.

Directions

1. In a wok or large skillet, stir-fry tofu until golden.
2. Add garlic, broccoli, bell pepper, and carrot; stir-fry until veggies are tender.
3. Pour in teriyaki sauce and toss to coat.
4. Serve over cooked rice.
5. Enjoy the savory delight of teriyaki tofu.

Chapter 4

Nutrient-Packed Breakfasts

2
servings

180
calories

5
minutes

Vegan Green Smoothie

Ingredients:

- 2 cups baby spinach
- 1 frozen banana
- 1/2 cup pineapple chunks
- 1/2 cup almond milk
- 1 tbsp chia seeds

A refreshing blend of greens and fruits to start your day.

Directions

1. Add spinach, frozen banana, pineapple chunks, almond milk, and chia seeds to a blender.
2. Blend until smooth.
3. Pour into glasses and sip your way to a nutrient-packed morning.

Substitutions

None

2
servings

320
calories

20
minutes

Vegan Spinach and Mushroom Breakfast Quesadilla

Ingredients:

- 2 whole wheat tortillas
- 1 cup baby spinach
- 1 cup sliced mushrooms
- 1/2 cup vegan cheese
- Olive oil for cooking

Substitutions

None

A savory quesadilla filled with spinach and mushrooms.

Directions

1. In a skillet, sauté mushrooms and spinach in olive oil until wilted.
2. Lay out tortillas, sprinkle with vegan cheese.
3. Add sautéed spinach and mushrooms.
4. Fold in half.
5. Cook until tortillas are crispy.
6. Slice and enjoy your wholesome breakfast quesadilla.

2
servings

250
calories

10
minutes

Vegan Coconut Chia Pudding

Ingredients:

- 1/4 cup chia seeds
- 1 cup coconut milk
- 1 tbsp maple syrup
- 1/2 tsp vanilla extract
- Fresh berries for topping

Substitutions

None

Creamy and satisfying, this chia pudding is a breakfast delight.

Directions

1. In a jar, mix chia seeds, coconut milk, maple syrup, and vanilla extract.
2. Stir well and refrigerate for at least 2 hours or overnight.
3. Top with fresh berries and dive into a creamy coconut morning treat.

2
servings

320
calories

15
minutes

Vegan Berry Protein Pancakes

Ingredients:

- 1 cup whole wheat flour
- 1 scoop vegan protein powder
- 1/2 cup mixed berries (blueberries, strawberries, etc.)
- 1 tsp baking powder
- 1 cup almond milk
- 1 tbsp maple syrup

Substitutions

None

Fluffy pancakes with a protein boost and a burst of berries.

Directions

1. In a bowl, mix flour, protein powder, mixed berries, and baking powder.
2. Add almond milk and maple syrup to achieve desired consistency.
3. Cook on a hot griddle until golden brown.
4. Stack 'em up and enjoy your protein-packed pancakes.

2
servings

280
calories

15
minutes

Vegan Breakfast Tacos

〰〰〰〰〰〰〰〰

Ingredients:

- 4 small whole wheat tortillas
- 1/2 block firm tofu, crumbled
- 1/2 cup bell peppers, diced
- 1/4 cup red onion, chopped
- 1/4 cup black beans, cooked
- 1/4 cup salsa
- Avocado slices for topping

Substitutions

None

Tacos for breakfast? Absolutely! Filled with tofu scramble and veggies.

Directions

1. In a skillet, sauté tofu, bell peppers, and red onion until tofu is heated through.
2. Warm tortillas in the skillet.
3. Fill tortillas with tofu scramble, black beans, salsa, and avocado slices.
4. Fold and enjoy your breakfast tacos with a Tex-Mex twist.

2
servings

220
calories

10
minutes

Vegan Mango and Kale Smoothie

Ingredients:

- 1 cup kale leaves, stems removed
- 1 ripe mango, peeled and chopped
- 1/2 cup coconut water
- 1/2 cup almond milk
- 1 tbsp honey (optional)

A tropical green smoothie with a sweet mango twist.

Directions

1. Add kale, mango, coconut water, almond milk, and honey (if using) to a blender.
2. Blend until smooth.
3. Pour into glasses and transport yourself to a tropical paradise with each sip.

Substitutions

Honey for sweetness

2
servings

260
calories

5
minutes

Vegan Peanut Butter and Banana Toast

Ingredients:

- 2 slices whole wheat bread
- 2 tbsp peanut butter
- 1 banana, sliced
- A drizzle of honey (optional)

Classic toast with a creamy peanut butter and banana topping.

Directions

1. Toast the bread until golden brown.
2. Spread peanut butter on each slice.
3. Top with banana slices.
4. Drizzle with honey if you like it sweet.
5. Savor the simple pleasure of peanut butter and banana on toast.

Substitutions

Honey for sweetness

2
servings

280
calories

20
minutes

Vegan Blueberry Buckwheat Pancakes

Ingredients:

- 1/2 cup buckwheat flour
- 1/2 cup almond milk
- 1/2 cup blueberries
- 1 tbsp maple syrup
- 1/2 tsp baking powder

Nutrient-rich buckwheat pancakes with a burst of blueberries.

Directions

1. In a bowl, combine buckwheat flour, almond milk, blueberries, maple syrup, and baking powder.
2. Mix until smooth.
3. Cook on a hot griddle until golden brown.
4. Serve with extra blueberries and a drizzle of maple syrup.
5. Enjoy the nutty goodness of buckwheat pancakes.

Substitutions

None

2
servings

240
calories

15
minutes

Vegan Tofu and Veggie Scramble

Ingredients:

- 1/2 block firm tofu, crumbled
- 1/2 cup bell peppers, diced
- 1/4 cup red onion, chopped
- 1/4 cup spinach leaves
- 1/4 tsp turmeric
- Salt and pepper to taste

Substitutions

None

A protein-packed scramble with tofu, veggies, and a hint of spice.

Directions

1. In a skillet, sauté crumbled tofu, bell peppers, and red onion until tofu is lightly browned.
2. Add spinach, turmeric, salt, and pepper; cook until spinach wilts.
3. Serve as a hearty breakfast scramble.
4. Enjoy your protein-packed morning.

2
servings

280
calories

10
minutes

Vegan Avocado Toast with Microgreens

Elevate your avocado toast with vibrant microgreens.

Ingredients:

- 2 slices whole wheat bread
- 1 ripe avocado
- 1/2 cup microgreens
- Lemon juice, salt, and pepper to taste

Directions

1. Toast the bread until golden brown.
2. Mash ripe avocado and spread it on each slice.
3. Drizzle with lemon juice and season with salt and pepper.
4. Top with a generous handful of microgreens.
5. Savor the flavors and textures of your elevated avocado toast.

Substitutions

None

Chapter 5
Wholesome Lunches

2
servings

380
calories

30
minutes

Vegan Falafel Bowl

A Mediterranean-inspired bowl with crispy falafel and fresh veggies.

Ingredients:

- 8 falafel patties (store-bought or homemade)
- 1 cup cooked quinoa
- 1 cup cherry tomatoes, halved
- 1/2 cucumber, sliced
- 1/2 cup Kalamata olives, pitted
- 1/4 cup red onion, thinly sliced
- Tahini dressing: 2 tbsp tahini, 2 tbsp lemon juice, 1 clove garlic, minced, water to thin

Directions

1. If using store-bought falafel, bake according to package instructions until crispy. If making homemade falafel, cook until golden brown.
2. In bowls, layer cooked quinoa, cherry tomatoes, cucumber, olives, red onion, and falafel.
3. Drizzle with tahini dressing, adding water to achieve desired consistency.
4. Enjoy your Mediterranean falafel bowl, packed with flavors.

Substitutions

None

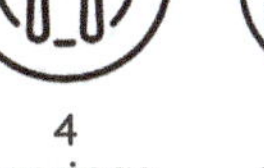

4
servings

320
calories

30
minutes

Vegan Roasted Vegetable and Quinoa Salad

A colorful salad bursting with roasted veggies and protein-packed quinoa.

Ingredients:

- 1 cup quinoa, cooked
- 2 cups mixed bell peppers, diced
- 1 cup zucchini, diced
- 1 cup cherry tomatoes, halved
- 1/4 cup red onion, thinly sliced
- 1/4 cup fresh basil leaves, chopped
- Balsamic vinaigrette: 2 tbsp balsamic vinegar, 1/4 cup olive oil, 1 clove garlic, minced, salt and pepper to taste

Directions

1. Preheat oven to 425°F (220°C).
2. Toss diced bell peppers, zucchini, and cherry tomatoes with olive oil, salt, and pepper.
3. Roast in the oven until veggies are tender and slightly caramelized.
4. In a large bowl, combine cooked quinoa, roasted veggies, red onion, and fresh basil.
5. Whisk together balsamic vinaigrette ingredients and drizzle over the salad.
6. Toss gently to coat.
7. Savor the flavors of this wholesome salad.

Substitutions

None

4 servings

250 calories

35 minutes

Vegan Minestrone Soup

Ingredients:

- 1 cup small pasta (such as ditalini or macaroni)
- 1 can cannellini beans, drained
- 1 can diced tomatoes
- 1 cup diced carrots
- 1 cup diced celery
- 1 cup diced zucchini
- 1/2 cup diced onion
- 2 cloves garlic, minced
- 4 cups vegetable broth
- 1 tsp dried basil
- 1 tsp dried oregano
- Salt and pepper to taste

Substitutions

None

A hearty and comforting Italian soup filled with veggies and beans.

Directions

1. In a large pot, sauté onions, garlic, carrots, celery, and zucchini until softened.
2. Add diced tomatoes, cannellini beans, vegetable broth, basil, oregano, salt, and pepper.
3. Simmer until veggies are tender.
4. In a separate pot, cook pasta according to package instructions.
5. Add cooked pasta to the soup.
6. Serve and enjoy this comforting minestrone soup.

4
servings

320
calories

25
minutes

Vegan Teriyaki Chickpea Stir-Fry

A quick and flavorful stir-fry with teriyaki chickpeas and crisp veggies.

Ingredients:

- 2 cups cooked brown rice
- 2 cans chickpeas, drained
- 1 cup broccoli florets
- 1 cup bell peppers, sliced
- 1/2 cup snap peas
- 1/4 cup green onions, chopped
- Teriyaki sauce: 1/4 cup soy sauce, 2 tbsp maple syrup, 1 tsp sesame oil, 1 clove garlic, minced, 1 tsp grated ginger, 1 tbsp cornstarch, water to thin

Directions

1. In a wok or large skillet, stir-fry chickpeas, broccoli, bell peppers, and snap peas until veggies are tender-crisp.
2. In a small bowl, whisk together the teriyaki sauce ingredients, adjusting the consistency with water.
3. Pour the teriyaki sauce over the stir-fry and toss to coat.
4. Serve the teriyaki chickpea stir-fry over cooked brown rice, garnished with chopped green onions.
5. Enjoy the savory goodness.

Substitutions

None

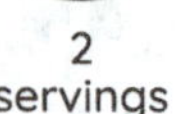

2
servings

320
calories

15
minutes

Vegan Mediterranean Wrap

Ingredients:

- 2 whole wheat tortillas
- 1 cup hummus
- 1 cup mixed greens
- 1/2 cup cherry tomatoes, halved
- 1/2 cucumber, sliced
- 1/4 cup Kalamata olives, pitted
- 1/4 cup red onion, thinly sliced
- 1/4 cup fresh parsley, chopped

A portable wrap filled with Mediterranean flavors and hummus.

Directions

1. Lay out tortillas and spread a generous layer of hummus on each.
2. Layer with mixed greens, cherry tomatoes, cucumber, olives, red onion, and fresh parsley.
3. Fold in the sides and roll up the wraps.
4. Slice in half for easy handling.
5. Enjoy your portable Mediterranean wrap bursting with flavors.

Substitutions

None

4
servings

230
calories

15
minutes

Vegan Black Bean and Corn Salad

Ingredients:

- 2 cans black beans, drained
- 2 cups corn kernels (fresh or frozen, thawed)
- 1 cup cherry tomatoes, halved
- 1/2 cup red bell pepper, diced
- 1/4 cup red onion, finely chopped
- Fresh cilantro for garnish
- Lime dressing: Juice of 2 limes, 2 tbsp olive oil, 1 clove garlic, minced, 1 tsp ground cumin, salt and pepper to taste

Substitutions

None

A vibrant salad with black beans, corn, and zesty lime dressing.

Directions

1. In a large bowl, combine black beans, corn, cherry tomatoes, red bell pepper, and red onion.
2. In a small bowl, whisk together the lime dressing ingredients.
3. Drizzle the dressing over the salad and toss to coat.
4. Garnish with fresh cilantro.
5. Savor the zesty flavors of this black bean and corn salad.

2
servings

300
calories

25
minutes

Vegan Sushi Bowl

All the flavors of sushi in a deconstructed bowl, perfect for lunch.

Ingredients:

- 1 cup sushi rice, cooked and seasoned with rice vinegar, sugar, and salt
- 1/2 cucumber, thinly sliced
- 1/2 avocado, sliced
- 1/2 cup carrots, julienned
- 1/2 cup nori seaweed, shredded
- Soy sauce and pickled ginger for serving

Directions

1. Divide the seasoned sushi rice between two bowls.
2. Arrange cucumber slices, avocado slices, julienned carrots, and shredded nori seaweed on top of the rice.
3. Serve with soy sauce and pickled ginger.
4. Enjoy the sushi experience in a convenient bowl form.

Substitutions

None

4
servings

280
calories

20
minutes

Vegan Greek Salad with Tofu Feta

Ingredients:

- 2 cups cucumber, diced
- 2 cups cherry tomatoes, halved
- 1/2 cup Kalamata olives, pitted
- 1/4 cup red onion, thinly sliced
- 1/4 cup fresh parsley, chopped
- Tofu feta: 1 block firm tofu, crumbled
- Juice of 1 lemon
- 2 tbsp olive oil
- 1 tsp dried oregano
- Salt and pepper to taste

Substitutions

None

A classic Greek salad with a vegan twist, featuring tofu feta.

Directions

1. In a large bowl, combine cucumber, cherry tomatoes, Kalamata olives, red onion, and fresh parsley.
2. In a separate bowl, prepare the tofu feta by mixing crumbled tofu, lemon juice, olive oil, dried oregano, salt, and pepper.
3. Gently toss the salad with the tofu feta mixture.
4. Enjoy the refreshing flavors of this Greek salad with a vegan twist.

4
servings

280
calories

25
minutes

Vegan Thai Coconut Soup

Ingredients:

- 1 can coconut milk
- 4 cups vegetable broth
- 1 cup mushrooms, sliced
- 1 cup bell peppers, sliced
- 1 cup tofu, cubed
- 2 tbsp red curry paste
- Juice of 1 lime
- Fresh cilantro for garnish

Substitutions

None

A fragrant and creamy Thai coconut soup with veggies and tofu.

Directions

1. In a pot, combine coconut milk and vegetable broth; bring to a simmer.
2. Stir in mushrooms, bell peppers, tofu, red curry paste, and lime juice.
3. Simmer until veggies are tender and tofu is heated through.
4. Serve with fresh cilantro garnish.
5. Enjoy the aromatic flavors of this Thai coconut soup.

2
servings

320
calories

30
minutes

Vegan Portobello Mushroom Burger

Ingredients:

- 2 large Portobello mushroom caps
- 2 whole wheat burger buns
- 1/2 cup baby spinach
- 1/2 cup roasted red bell pepper, sliced
- 1/4 cup red onion, thinly sliced
- 1/4 cup balsamic glaze
- Olive oil for grilling mushrooms

Substitutions

None

A hearty burger with marinated Portobello mushrooms as the star.

Directions

1. Preheat grill or grill pan.
2. Brush Portobello mushroom caps with olive oil and grill until tender, about 4-5 minutes per side.
3. Assemble burgers with baby spinach, roasted red bell pepper, and red onion on whole wheat buns.
4. Drizzle with balsamic glaze.
5. Enjoy your hearty Portobello mushroom burger.

We have a small favor to ask

As we delve deeper into the realm of "Vegan Superfood," exploring the nourishing and vibrant world of plant-based superfoods, I want to take a moment to express my heartfelt gratitude to all of you, the intrepid seekers of healthier and more wholesome eating. Together, we've embarked on a journey to discover the delicious and transformative power of plant-based superfoods.

Now, in the midst of this culinary adventure, I have a humble request. In the world of small publishers like us, reviews are akin to the nutrients that sustain our culinary creations – they are the vital essence that keeps our passion alive and thriving.

If you've found inspiration in our collection of plant-based superfood recipes, if you've marveled at the incredible flavors and health benefits these ingredients bring to your table, I kindly ask for your support. Please take a moment to revisit the app or website where you acquired this book, where you'll discover that cherished review button. There, you can bestow upon us a rating and share a brief sentence or two about your experience.

Your review isn't just feedback; it's a connection, a beacon that guides fellow health-conscious food enthusiasts to these pages. It strengthens our mission to make plant-based superfood dining accessible and mouthwateringly delightful. Every review you leave is like a sprinkle of chia seeds, adding nourishment to our passion for this culinary journey. Rest assured, we read each one with genuine appreciation and anticipation.

And if, by any chance, you've noticed a minor hiccup or oversight along the way, please understand that we've poured our heart and soul into crafting this superfood adventure. We've aimed for perfection, but even the most meticulous chefs can sometimes overlook a detail in the hustle and bustle of the kitchen. Your understanding is the gentle reminder to savor the journey rather than obsess over the destination.

So, as we return to the recipes, invigorated by the energy of plant-based superfoods, let's continue to savor the art of nourishing and flavorful eating. Until our paths cross again amidst the vibrant colors of fresh produce and the zest of superfood smoothies, stay curious, keep experimenting, and revel in the joy of every superfood-infused bite. Your culinary journey continues, and we're profoundly grateful to have been a part of it.

Chapter 6
Flavorful Dinners

4
servings

340
calories

30
minutes

Vegan Cauliflower Alfredo Pasta

Creamy and comforting cauliflower alfredo sauce over pasta.

Ingredients:

- 8 oz (about 2 cups) pasta (gluten-free if desired)
- 1 small head cauliflower, chopped
- 3 cloves garlic, minced
- 1 cup unsweetened almond milk
- 1/4 cup nutritional yeast
- 2 tbsp olive oil
- Salt and pepper to taste

Directions

1. Cook pasta according to package instructions until al dente.
2. While pasta is cooking, steam cauliflower until tender.
3. In a blender, combine steamed cauliflower, minced garlic, almond milk, nutritional yeast, olive oil, salt, and pepper.
4. Blend until smooth and creamy.
5. Drain pasta and return it to the pot.
6. Pour the cauliflower alfredo sauce over the pasta.
7. Toss to coat and warm through.
8. Serve your creamy cauliflower alfredo pasta with a sprinkle of nutritional yeast.
9. Indulge in the lusciousness of this guilt-free comfort food.

Substitutions

None

4
servings

320
calories

40
minutes

Vegan Sweet Potato and Lentil Curry

Ingredients:

- 1 cup dried green or brown lentils, rinsed
- 2 large sweet potatoes, peeled and diced
- 1 onion, chopped
- 3 cloves garlic, minced
- 1 can diced tomatoes
- 1 can coconut milk
- 2 tbsp curry powder
- 1 tsp cumin
- Salt and pepper to taste

Substitutions

None

A hearty curry featuring sweet potatoes and protein-rich lentils.

Directions

1. In a large pot, sauté onions and garlic until fragrant.
2. Add sweet potatoes, lentils, diced tomatoes, coconut milk, curry powder, cumin, salt, and pepper.
3. Simmer until sweet potatoes are tender and lentils are cooked.
4. Serve your sweet potato and lentil curry over rice or quinoa.
5. Enjoy the warm and hearty flavors of this comforting dish.

4
servings

280
calories

30
minutes

Vegan Mexican Quinoa Bowl

Ingredients:

- 1 cup quinoa, cooked
- 1 can black beans, drained
- 1 cup corn kernels (fresh or frozen, thawed)
- 1 cup cherry tomatoes, halved
- 1/2 cup red onion, finely chopped
- 1 avocado, sliced
- Fresh cilantro for garnish
- Lime wedges for serving

Substitutions

None

A colorful and nutritious bowl with quinoa, black beans, and avocado.

Directions

1. In bowls, layer cooked quinoa, black beans, corn, cherry tomatoes, red onion, and avocado.
2. Garnish with fresh cilantro.
3. Serve with lime wedges for squeezing over the bowl.
4. Enjoy the vibrant and wholesome flavors of this Mexican-inspired quinoa bowl.

4
servings

200
calories

45
minutes

Vegan Ratatouille

A French classic with layers of sliced vegetables in tomato sauce.

Ingredients:

- 1 large eggplant, sliced
- 2 large zucchinis, sliced
- 2 large tomatoes, sliced
- 1 large red bell pepper, sliced
- 1 large yellow bell pepper, sliced
- 1 onion, thinly sliced
- 3 cloves garlic, minced
- 1 can crushed tomatoes
- 2 tbsp olive oil
- 1 tsp dried thyme
- 1 tsp dried oregano
- Salt and pepper to taste

Substitutions

None

Directions

1. Preheat oven to 375°F (190°C).
2. In a large baking dish, layer sliced eggplant, zucchinis, tomatoes, red bell pepper, yellow bell pepper, onion, and minced garlic.
3. Pour crushed tomatoes over the layered vegetables.
4. Drizzle with olive oil and sprinkle with dried thyme, dried oregano, salt, and pepper.
5. Cover with foil and bake for 30 minutes.
6. Uncover and bake for an additional 15 minutes, until veggies are tender and slightly caramelized.
7. Serve your ratatouille as a flavorful side or over cooked quinoa or rice.
8. Enjoy this elegant French dish bursting with Mediterranean flavors.

4 servings | **340 calories** | **35 minutes**

Vegan Black Bean Enchiladas

Spicy black bean enchiladas topped with zesty enchilada sauce and vegan cheese.

Ingredients:

- 8 whole wheat tortillas
- 2 cans black beans, drained
- 1 cup corn kernels
- 1 cup diced tomatoes
- 1/2 cup diced onion
- 2 cloves garlic, minced
- 1 tsp chili powder
- 1/2 tsp cumin
- 1 can enchilada sauce
- 1 cup vegan shredded cheese
- Fresh cilantro for garnish

Directions

1. Preheat oven to 375°F (190°C).
2. In a large skillet, sauté onions and garlic until fragrant.
3. Add black beans, corn, diced tomatoes, chili powder, and cumin; cook until heated through.
4. Pour a small amount of enchilada sauce into the bottom of a baking dish.
5. Fill tortillas with the black bean mixture, roll them up, and place them seam-side down in the baking dish.
6. Pour the remaining enchilada sauce over the rolled enchiladas.
7. Sprinkle vegan shredded cheese on top.
8. Bake for 20 minutes, until cheese is bubbly and golden.
9. Garnish with fresh cilantro before serving.
10. Enjoy these spicy and cheesy black bean enchiladas.

Substitutions

None

4
servings

320
calories

20
minutes

Vegan Spaghetti Aglio e Olio

Ingredients:

- 8 oz (about 2 cups) spaghetti (gluten-free if desired)
- 6 cloves garlic, thinly sliced
- 1/4 cup olive oil
- 1/2 tsp red pepper flakes (adjust to taste)
- Fresh parsley, chopped, for garnish

Substitutions

None

A simple yet elegant pasta dish with garlic, olive oil, and red pepper flakes.

Directions

1. Cook pasta according to package instructions until al dente.
2. In a large skillet, sauté garlic and red pepper flakes in olive oil until garlic is golden and fragrant.
3. Drain cooked pasta and add it to the skillet.
4. Toss to coat the pasta with the garlic-infused olive oil.
5. Garnish with fresh parsley.
6. Serve your spaghetti aglio e olio with a sprinkle of red pepper flakes for extra heat, if desired.
7. Enjoy the simplicity and bold flavors of this Italian classic.

4
servings

260
calories

30
minutes

Vegan Lemon Herb Tofu

Ingredients:

- 1 block firm tofu, sliced into rectangles
- Zest and juice of 1 lemon
- 2 cloves garlic, minced
- 2 tbsp fresh herbs (such as parsley, thyme, or rosemary), chopped
- 2 tbsp olive oil
- Salt and pepper to taste

Substitutions

None

Tangy and herb-infused tofu, perfect for a light and flavorful dinner.

Directions

1. In a bowl, combine lemon zest, lemon juice, minced garlic, chopped fresh herbs, olive oil, salt, and pepper.
2. Place tofu slices in a shallow dish and pour the marinade over them.
3. Marinate for at least 15 minutes, flipping tofu halfway through.
4. Heat a skillet over medium-high heat and add tofu slices.
5. Cook until tofu is golden brown and slightly crispy on both sides.
6. Serve your lemon herb tofu with your choice of side dishes.
7. Enjoy the zesty and aromatic flavors of this tofu dish.

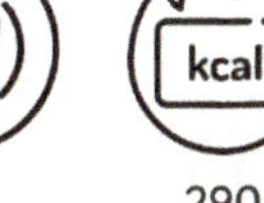

4
servings

290
calories

45
minutes

Vegan Mushroom and Spinach Stuffed Bell Peppers

Ingredients:

- 4 large bell peppers, tops removed and seeds removed
- 1 cup quinoa, cooked
- 2 cups mushrooms, chopped
- 2 cups baby spinach, chopped
- 1 onion, chopped
- 2 cloves garlic, minced
- 1 can diced tomatoes
- 1/2 cup vegetable broth
- 2 tbsp olive oil
- 1 tsp dried thyme
- 1 tsp dried oregano
- Salt and pepper to taste

Substitutions

None

Bell peppers stuffed with a savory mixture of mushrooms and spinach.

Directions

1. Preheat oven to 375°F (190°C).
2. In a large skillet, sauté onions and garlic until fragrant.
3. Add mushrooms and cook until they release their moisture and become tender.
4. Add baby spinach and cook until wilted.
5. Stir in cooked quinoa, diced tomatoes, vegetable broth, dried thyme, dried oregano, salt, and pepper.
6. Stuff the mixture into the hollowed bell peppers.
7. Place stuffed peppers in a baking dish and drizzle with olive oil.
8. Cover with foil and bake for 30 minutes.
9. Uncover and bake for an additional 15 minutes, until peppers are tender.
10. Serve your mushroom and spinach stuffed bell peppers.
11. Enjoy the comforting and wholesome flavors of this dish.

 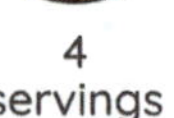  

4
servings

280
calories

40
minutes

Vegan Indian Dahl

A flavorful and comforting Indian lentil stew, perfect with rice or naan.

Ingredients:

- 1 cup red lentils, rinsed
- 1 onion, chopped
- 2 cloves garlic, minced
- 1 tbsp ginger, minced
- 1 can diced tomatoes
- 2 cups vegetable broth
- 1 can coconut milk
- 1 tsp curry powder
- 1/2 tsp turmeric
- 1/2 tsp cumin
- 1/2 tsp garam masala
- Salt and pepper to taste

Directions

1. In a large pot, sauté onions, garlic, and ginger until fragrant.
2. Add diced tomatoes, red lentils, vegetable broth, coconut milk, curry powder, turmeric, cumin, garam masala, salt, and pepper.
3. Simmer until lentils are tender and the stew has thickened.
4. Serve your Indian dahl over rice or with naan bread.
5. Enjoy the rich and aromatic flavors of this Indian comfort food.

Substitutions

None

4 servings

260 calories

50 minutes

Vegan Mediterranean Stuffed Eggplant

Eggplants stuffed with a Mediterranean mixture of quinoa and veggies.

Ingredients:

- 2 large eggplants
- 1 cup quinoa, cooked
- 1 cup cherry tomatoes, halved
- 1/2 cup Kalamata olives, pitted and chopped
- 1/2 cup red onion, finely chopped
- 1/4 cup fresh parsley, chopped
- Juice of 1 lemon
- 2 tbsp olive oil
- Salt and pepper to taste

Directions

1. Preheat oven to 375°F (190°C).
2. Cut eggplants in half lengthwise and scoop out the flesh, leaving a shell.
3. Chop the scooped-out eggplant flesh.
4. In a skillet, sauté chopped eggplant flesh until tender.
5. In a bowl, combine cooked quinoa, sautéed eggplant, cherry tomatoes, Kalamata olives, red onion, fresh parsley, lemon juice, olive oil, salt, and pepper.
6. Fill the eggplant shells with the quinoa mixture.
7. Place stuffed eggplants in a baking dish and cover with foil.
8. Bake for 30 minutes.
9. Uncover and bake for an additional 10-15 minutes, until eggplants are tender and slightly golden.
10. Serve your Mediterranean stuffed eggplants as a wholesome dinner option.
11. Enjoy the vibrant flavors of this dish.

Substitutions

None

Chapter 7
Supercharged Breakfasts

2
servings

240
calories

10
minutes

Vegan Spirulina Smoothie

A vibrant and supercharged smoothie featuring spirulina, a nutrient powerhouse.

Ingredients:

- 2 ripe bananas
- 2 cups unsweetened almond milk
- 1 tsp spirulina powder
- 1 tbsp chia seeds
- 1 tbsp maple syrup (optional)
- Fresh berries for topping

Directions

1. In a blender, combine ripe bananas, almond milk, spirulina powder, chia seeds, and maple syrup (if desired).
2. Blend until smooth and creamy.
3. Pour into glasses and top with fresh berries for added antioxidants and flavor.
4. Sip on your supercharged spirulina smoothie and embrace the vibrant green goodness.

Substitutions

Maple syrup can be substituted with agave syrup or date syrup.

2
servings

380
calories

15
minutes

Vegan Superfood Breakfast Bowl

A nutrient-packed breakfast bowl filled with superfoods and vibrant colors.

Ingredients:

- 1 cup cooked quinoa
- 1 cup mixed berries (such as blueberries, strawberries, and raspberries)
- 1/2 cup sliced kiwi
- 1/4 cup chopped nuts (almonds, walnuts, or pecans)
- 2 tbsp hemp seeds
- 2 tbsp pure maple syrup
- 1/2 tsp cinnamon

Directions

1. Divide cooked quinoa into bowls.
2. Arrange mixed berries, sliced kiwi, and chopped nuts on top.
3. Sprinkle with hemp seeds.
4. Drizzle with pure maple syrup and sprinkle with cinnamon.
5. Enjoy your nutrient-packed superfood breakfast bowl, bursting with colors and flavors.

Substitutions

None

2
servings

280
calories

15
minutes

Vegan Pumpkin Spice Oatmeal

Ingredients:

- 1 cup rolled oats
- 2 cups unsweetened almond milk
- 1/2 cup canned pumpkin puree
- 2 tbsp maple syrup
- 1 tsp pumpkin pie spice
- 1/4 cup chopped pecans
- 1/4 cup dried cranberries

Substitutions

None

A comforting bowl of oatmeal with the warm flavors of pumpkin spice.

Directions

1. In a saucepan, combine rolled oats and almond milk.
2. Stir in pumpkin puree, maple syrup, and pumpkin pie spice.
3. Cook over medium heat until oats are tender and the mixture is creamy, about 10 minutes.
4. Serve your pumpkin spice oatmeal in bowls, topped with chopped pecans and dried cranberries for added crunch and sweetness.
5. Enjoy the cozy and seasonal flavors of this oatmeal.

2
servings

320
calories

20
minutes

Vegan Matcha Pancakes

Ingredients:

- 1 cup all-purpose flour
- 1 tbsp matcha powder
- 2 tbsp sugar
- 1 tsp baking powder
- 1/2 tsp baking soda
- 1 cup unsweetened almond milk
- 1 tsp vanilla extract
- 1 tbsp apple cider vinegar
- Fresh berries for topping

Substitutions

None

Fluffy green matcha pancakes infused with antioxidant-rich matcha powder.

Directions

1. In a mixing bowl, whisk together all-purpose flour, matcha powder, sugar, baking powder, and baking soda.
2. In a separate bowl, combine almond milk, vanilla extract, and apple cider vinegar. Let it sit for a few minutes to curdle.
3. Pour the wet mixture into the dry mixture and whisk until well combined.
4. Heat a non-stick skillet over medium heat and lightly grease it.
5. Pour ladlefuls of pancake batter onto the skillet and cook until bubbles form on the surface.
6. Flip the pancakes and cook until golden brown on both sides.
7. Serve your matcha pancakes with fresh berries on top.
8. Enjoy these fluffy and vibrant green pancakes for a morning boost.

2
servings

260
calories

5
minutes

Vegan Almond Butter Toast with Berries

Simple and satisfying almond butter toast topped with fresh berries.

Ingredients:

- 4 slices whole wheat bread
- 1/2 cup almond butter
- 1 cup mixed berries (such as strawberries, blueberries, and blackberries)
- Drizzle of honey or maple syrup (optional)

Directions

1. Toast slices of whole wheat bread until golden brown.
2. Spread almond butter generously on each slice.
3. Top with mixed berries.
4. Drizzle with honey or maple syrup if desired for a touch of sweetness.
5. Enjoy your quick and nutritious almond butter toast with the vibrant flavors of fresh berries.

Substitutions

Honey or maple syrup can be omitted for a less sweet option.

2
servings

300
calories

10
minutes

Vegan Chocolate Avocado Smoothie

Ingredients:

- 1 ripe avocado
- 2 cups unsweetened almond milk
- 2 tbsp cocoa powder
- 2 tbsp pure maple syrup
- 1/2 tsp vanilla extract
- 1/4 cup oats
- 1/2 banana (frozen for creaminess)
- Pinch of salt

A creamy and indulgent chocolate smoothie with the goodness of avocado.

Directions

1. In a blender, combine ripe avocado, almond milk, cocoa powder, pure maple syrup, vanilla extract, oats, banana, and a pinch of salt.
2. Blend until smooth and creamy.
3. Pour into glasses and enjoy your creamy chocolate avocado smoothie, a guilt-free treat packed with nutrients.

Substitutions

None

2
servings

290
calories

15
minutes

Vegan Turmeric Tofu Scramble

Ingredients:

- 1 block firm tofu, crumbled
- 1/2 cup diced bell peppers
- 1/2 cup diced onions
- 2 cloves garlic, minced
- 1 tsp turmeric powder
- 1/2 tsp cumin
- 1/4 tsp paprika
- Salt and pepper to taste
- Fresh cilantro for garnish

Substitutions

None

A vibrant tofu scramble with the anti-inflammatory benefits of turmeric.

Directions

1. In a skillet, sauté diced bell peppers and onions until softened.
2. Add minced garlic, crumbled tofu, turmeric powder, cumin, paprika, salt, and pepper.
3. Cook, stirring occasionally, until tofu is heated through and seasoned.
4. Garnish with fresh cilantro.
5. Serve your turmeric tofu scramble as a hearty and nutritious breakfast option.
6. Enjoy the golden hues and flavors of this vibrant scramble.

2
servings

280
calories

15
minutes

Vegan Blue Spirulina Smoothie Bowl

Ingredients:

- 2 frozen bananas
- 1 tsp blue spirulina powder
- 1/2 cup unsweetened coconut milk
- 1/2 cup frozen pineapple chunks
- 1/2 cup frozen mango chunks
- Fresh fruit, coconut flakes, and chia seeds for topping

Substitutions

None

A visually stunning smoothie bowl featuring blue spirulina and tropical fruits.

Directions

1. In a blender, combine frozen bananas, blue spirulina powder, coconut milk, frozen pineapple, and frozen mango.
2. Blend until smooth and creamy.
3. Pour into bowls and top with fresh fruit, coconut flakes, and chia seeds for added texture and nutrients.
4. Savor the tropical vibes and vibrant colors of your blue spirulina smoothie bowl.

2
servings

280
calories

15
minutes

Vegan Goji Berry Porridge

Ingredients:

- 1 cup rolled oats
- 2 cups unsweetened almond milk
- 1/4 cup dried goji berries
- 2 tbsp pure maple syrup
- 1 tsp vanilla extract
- Pinch of salt
- Fresh berries for topping

Substitutions

None

A nourishing porridge infused with the sweetness and antioxidants of goji berries.

Directions

1. In a saucepan, combine rolled oats, almond milk, dried goji berries, pure maple syrup, vanilla extract, and a pinch of salt.
2. Cook over medium heat until oats are tender and the mixture is creamy, about 10 minutes.
3. Serve your goji berry porridge in bowls, topped with fresh berries for added antioxidants and flavor.
4. Enjoy this wholesome and naturally sweetened breakfast option.

12
cookies

120
calories

25
minutes

Vegan Hemp Seed Breakfast Cookies

Nutrient-packed breakfast cookies with the crunch of hemp seeds and dried fruits.

Ingredients:

- 1 cup rolled oats
- 1/2 cup almond flour
- 1/4 cup hemp seeds
- 1/4 cup dried cranberries
- 1/4 cup dried apricots, chopped
- 1/4 cup pure maple syrup
- 1/4 cup almond butter
- 1 tsp vanilla extract
- Pinch of salt

Directions

1. Preheat your oven to 350°F (175°C) and line a baking sheet with parchment paper.
2. In a mixing bowl, combine rolled oats, almond flour, hemp seeds, dried cranberries, and chopped dried apricots.
3. In a separate bowl, whisk together pure maple syrup, almond butter, vanilla extract, and a pinch of salt.
4. Pour the wet mixture over the dry mixture and stir until well combined.
5. Drop spoonfuls of the cookie dough onto the prepared baking sheet.
6. Flatten each cookie slightly with the back of a fork.
7. Bake for 12-15 minutes, or until the cookies are lightly golden.
8. Let them cool on a wire rack.
9. Enjoy your homemade hemp seed breakfast cookies as a convenient and nutritious morning treat.

Substitutions

None

Chapter 8
Nourishing Lunches

4
servings

320
calories

20
minutes

Vegan Quinoa and Chickpea Salad

Ingredients:

- 1 cup quinoa, cooked
- 1 can chickpeas, drained
- 1 cup cherry tomatoes, halved
- 1 cucumber, diced
- 1/4 cup red onion, finely chopped
- 1/4 cup fresh parsley, chopped
- Juice of 2 lemons
- 2 tbsp olive oil
- Salt and pepper to taste

Substitutions

None

A hearty salad with quinoa, chickpeas, and a zesty vinaigrette dressing.

Directions

1. In a large bowl, combine cooked quinoa, chickpeas, cherry tomatoes, cucumber, red onion, and fresh parsley.
2. In a small bowl, whisk together lemon juice, olive oil, salt, and pepper.
3. Drizzle the dressing over the salad and toss to coat.
4. Serve your quinoa and chickpea salad as a nourishing and filling lunch option.
5. Enjoy the vibrant flavors and textures of this wholesome dish.

4
servings

220
calories

30
minutes

Vegan Broccoli and Cashew Soup

Creamy and nutritious broccoli soup with a hint of richness from cashews.

Ingredients:

- 4 cups broccoli florets
- 1 cup cashews, soaked
- 1 onion, chopped
- 2 cloves garlic, minced
- 4 cups vegetable broth
- 1 cup unsweetened almond milk
- 1 tbsp nutritional yeast
- Salt and pepper to taste

Directions

1. In a large pot, sauté onions and garlic until translucent.
2. Add broccoli florets and sauté for a few more minutes.
3. Drain and rinse cashews, then add them to the pot along with vegetable broth.
4. Simmer until broccoli is tender.
5. Use an immersion blender to puree the soup until smooth.
6. Stir in almond milk and nutritional yeast.
7. Season with salt and pepper.
8. Serve your creamy broccoli and cashew soup as a comforting and nutritious lunch.
9. Enjoy the velvety texture and rich flavors of this soup.

Substitutions

None

2
servings

350
calories

30
minutes

Vegan BBQ Tempeh Sandwich

A savory and smoky BBQ tempeh sandwich with all the fixings.

Ingredients:

- 1 package tempeh, sliced
- 1/2 cup BBQ sauce
- 4 whole wheat burger buns
- 1 cup coleslaw mix
- 1/4 cup vegan mayo
- 1 tsp apple cider vinegar
- 1 tsp agave syrup
- Salt and pepper to taste

Directions

1. Marinate tempeh slices in BBQ sauce for at least 15 minutes.
2. Heat a skillet over medium heat and cook tempeh slices until browned and heated through.
3. In a bowl, combine coleslaw mix, vegan mayo, apple cider vinegar, agave syrup, salt, and pepper to make coleslaw.
4. Toast burger buns.
5. Assemble your BBQ tempeh sandwiches with a generous layer of coleslaw.
6. Enjoy these savory and satisfying sandwiches packed with flavor.

Substitutions

None

4
servings

290
calories

25
minutes

Vegan Mediterranean Couscous Salad

A refreshing salad with couscous, Mediterranean veggies, and a lemon herb dressing.

Ingredients:

- 1 cup couscous, cooked
- 1 cup cucumber, diced
- 1 cup cherry tomatoes, halved
- 1/2 cup Kalamata olives, pitted and chopped
- 1/4 cup red onion, finely chopped
- 1/4 cup fresh parsley, chopped
- Juice of 2 lemons
- 2 tbsp olive oil
- 1 tsp dried oregano
- Salt and pepper to taste

Directions

1. In a large bowl, combine cooked couscous, cucumber, cherry tomatoes, Kalamata olives, red onion, and fresh parsley.
2. In a small bowl, whisk together lemon juice, olive oil, dried oregano, salt, and pepper.
3. Drizzle the dressing over the salad and toss to combine.
4. Serve your Mediterranean couscous salad as a light and refreshing lunch option.
5. Enjoy the Mediterranean flavors and textures of this delightful salad.

Substitutions

None

4
servings

380
calories

20
minutes

Vegan Thai Peanut Noodles

Ingredients:

- 8 oz (about 2 cups) rice noodles (gluten-free if desired)
- 1 cup broccoli florets
- 1 red bell pepper, thinly sliced
- 1 carrot, julienned
- 1/2 cup snap peas, sliced
- 1/4 cup green onions, chopped
- 1/4 cup peanuts, chopped
- Fresh cilantro for garnish

Substitutions

Rice noodles can be substituted with your favorite type of noodles.

Creamy and flavorful Thai peanut noodles with a medley of veggies.

Directions

1. Cook rice noodles according to package instructions until al dente.
2. In a large skillet, stir-fry broccoli florets, red bell pepper, carrot, and snap peas until tender.
3. In a bowl, whisk together the peanut sauce ingredients (see below).
4. Toss cooked noodles and stir-fried veggies with the peanut sauce until well coated.
5. Serve your Thai peanut noodles garnished with chopped peanuts and fresh cilantro.
6. Enjoy the creamy and spicy flavors of this Thai-inspired dish.

Peanut Sauce:

- 1/4 cup peanut butter
- 2 tbsp soy sauce (or tamari for gluten-free)
- 2 tbsp rice vinegar
- 2 tbsp maple syrup
- 1 tsp sriracha sauce (adjust to taste)
- 1 clove garlic, minced
- 1 tsp grated ginger

4
servings

290
calories

45
minutes

Vegan Mexican Stuffed Peppers

Bell peppers stuffed with a flavorful mixture of rice, beans, and spices.

Ingredients:

- 4 large bell peppers, tops removed and seeds removed
- 1 cup cooked rice
- 1 can black beans, drained and rinsed
- 1 cup corn kernels (fresh or frozen)
- 1 cup diced tomatoes (canned or fresh)
- 1/2 cup red onion, finely chopped
- 2 cloves garlic, minced
- 1 tsp chili powder
- 1 tsp cumin
- Salt and pepper to taste
- 1 cup vegan shredded cheese (optional)

Substitutions

Vegan shredded cheese can be omitted or substituted with nutritional yeast for a cheesy flavor.

Directions

1. Preheat oven to 375°F (190°C).
2. In a large bowl, combine cooked rice, black beans, corn kernels, diced tomatoes, red onion, minced garlic, chili powder, cumin, salt, and pepper.
3. Stuff the mixture into the hollowed bell peppers.
4. Place stuffed peppers in a baking dish and cover with foil.
5. Bake for 30 minutes.
6. Remove the foil and bake for an additional 15 minutes, until peppers are tender.
7. If desired, sprinkle vegan shredded cheese on top of the peppers and bake for a few more minutes until it melts.
8. Serve your Mexican stuffed peppers as a hearty and satisfying lunch.
9. Enjoy the fiesta of flavors in every bite.

4
servings

320
calories

30
minutes

Vegan Jackfruit Tacos

Flavor-packed vegan tacos featuring jackfruit, a fantastic meat substitute.

Ingredients:

- 2 cans young green jackfruit in water or brine, drained and shredded
- 1 onion, chopped
- 2 cloves garlic, minced
- 1 can diced tomatoes
- 2 tbsp chili powder
- 1 tsp cumin
- 1/2 tsp smoked paprika
- Salt and pepper to taste
- 8 small corn tortillas
- Toppings: diced avocado, chopped cilantro, vegan sour cream

Directions

1. In a skillet, sauté chopped onions and garlic until fragrant.
2. Add shredded jackfruit, diced tomatoes, chili powder, cumin, smoked paprika, salt, and pepper.
3. Cook until jackfruit is tender and the mixture is heated through.
4. Warm corn tortillas in a dry skillet or microwave.
5. Assemble your jackfruit tacos with the flavorful filling and your choice of toppings.
6. Enjoy these savory and satisfying tacos with a meaty twist.

Substitutions

None

4
servings

260
calories

20
minutes

Vegan Kale Caesar Salad

Ingredients:

- 1 bunch kale, stems removed and leaves torn into bite-sized pieces
- 1 cup croutons (store-bought or homemade)
- 1/4 cup vegan Caesar dressing
- 1/4 cup vegan parmesan cheese
- Juice of 1 lemon
- Salt and pepper to taste

Substitutions

None

A modern twist on the classic Caesar salad, featuring kale and a creamy vegan dressing.

Directions

1. In a large bowl, massage torn kale leaves with lemon juice, salt, and pepper until slightly softened.
2. Toss with croutons, vegan Caesar dressing, and vegan parmesan cheese.
3. Serve your kale Caesar salad as a refreshing and nutritious lunch option.
4. Enjoy the modern twist on this classic salad with all the creamy goodness.

4
servings

260
calories

40
minutes

Vegan Mushroom and Wild Rice Soup

Ingredients:

- 1 cup wild rice, cooked
- 8 oz mushrooms, sliced
- 1 onion, chopped
- 2 cloves garlic, minced
- 4 cups vegetable broth
- 1 cup unsweetened almond milk
- 2 tbsp olive oil
- 1 tsp dried thyme
- Salt and pepper to taste

Substitutions

None

A hearty soup with a blend of mushrooms and nutty wild rice in a flavorful broth.

Directions

1. In a large pot, sauté chopped onions and garlic in olive oil until translucent.
2. Add sliced mushrooms and dried thyme, then sauté until mushrooms are tender.
3. Pour in vegetable broth and almond milk.
4. Add cooked wild rice, salt, and pepper.
5. Simmer for about 20-25 minutes until flavors meld together.
6. Serve your mushroom and wild rice soup as a hearty and comforting lunch.
7. Enjoy the earthy and nutty notes of this satisfying soup.

4
servings

350
calories

30
minutes

Vegan Portobello Burger with Guacamole

Ingredients:

- 4 large Portobello mushrooms, stems removed
- 4 whole wheat burger buns
- 1 cup cherry tomatoes, halved
- 1/4 cup red onion, finely chopped
- 1/4 cup fresh basil leaves
- 2 cloves garlic, minced
- Juice of 1 lemon
- 1 tbsp olive oil
- Salt and pepper to taste

Substitutions

None

A juicy Portobello mushroom burger topped with creamy guacamole.

Directions

1. Preheat grill or grill pan to medium-high heat.
2. In a bowl, combine cherry tomatoes, red onion, fresh basil leaves, minced garlic, lemon juice, olive oil, salt, and pepper to make a salsa.
3. Grill Portobello mushrooms for about 5-7 minutes on each side until tender and grill marks appear.
4. Toast burger buns on the grill.
5. Assemble your Portobello burgers with a grilled mushroom, a generous spoonful of salsa, and your choice of toppings.
6. Serve your Portobello burger with guacamole as a satisfying and flavorful lunch option.
7. Enjoy the savory and smoky goodness of this burger.

Chapter 9
Satisfying Dinners

4
servings

320
calories

40
minutes

Vegan Spaghetti Squash Pad Thai

A low-carb twist on classic Pad Thai, using spaghetti squash as the base.

Ingredients:

- 1 large spaghetti squash, halved and seeded
- 1 cup carrots, julienned
- 1 cup bell peppers, thinly sliced
- 1 cup snap peas, sliced
- 1/2 cup green onions, chopped
- 1/2 cup peanuts, chopped
- 1/4 cup fresh cilantro, chopped
- Lime wedges for garnish

Pad Thai Sauce:
- 1/4 cup soy sauce (or tamari for gluten-free)
- 2 tbsp maple syrup
- Juice of 2 limes
- 2 cloves garlic, minced
- 1 tsp grated ginger

Substitutions

Tamari can be used for a gluten-free version.

Directions

1. Preheat the oven to 375°F (190°C).
2. Place spaghetti squash halves cut-side down on a baking sheet and roast for 30-40 minutes until the flesh is tender and easily shreds into "noodles" with a fork.
3. While the squash is roasting, whisk together all the Pad Thai sauce ingredients in a bowl.
4. Heat a large skillet over medium heat and add carrots, bell peppers, and snap peas. Sauté until slightly softened.
5. Shred the roasted spaghetti squash into "noodles" with a fork and add them to the skillet.
6. Pour the Pad Thai sauce over the vegetables and squash. Toss to coat.
7. Cook for an additional 5 minutes to heat everything through.
8. Serve your spaghetti squash Pad Thai garnished with green onions, chopped peanuts, fresh cilantro, and lime wedges.
9. Enjoy this low-carb twist on a Thai favorite.

4
servings

330
calories

40
minutes

Vegan Chickpea and Sweet Potato Curry

Ingredients:

- 2 cups cooked brown rice
- 2 cups sweet potatoes, peeled and diced
- 1 can chickpeas, drained and rinsed
- 1 onion, chopped
- 2 cloves garlic, minced
- 1 can diced tomatoes
- 1 can coconut milk
- 2 tbsp curry powder
- 1 tsp ground turmeric
- Salt and pepper to taste
- Fresh cilantro for garnish

Substitutions

None

A comforting and flavorful curry with chickpeas and sweet potatoes, served with rice.

Directions

1. In a large pot, sauté chopped onions and garlic until fragrant.
2. Add diced sweet potatoes and continue to sauté for a few minutes.
3. Stir in curry powder, ground turmeric, salt, and pepper.
4. Pour in diced tomatoes, coconut milk, and chickpeas.
5. Simmer for about 20-25 minutes until sweet potatoes are tender.
6. Serve your chickpea and sweet potato curry over cooked brown rice.
7. Garnish with fresh cilantro.
8. Enjoy this comforting and nourishing curry.

4
servings

280
calories

45
minutes

Vegan Quinoa-Stuffed Acorn Squash

Roasted acorn squash halves stuffed with quinoa, veggies, and herbs.

Ingredients:

- 2 acorn squash, halved and seeds removed
- 1 cup quinoa, cooked
- 1 cup diced butternut squash
- 1/2 cup diced red bell pepper
- 1/2 cup diced red onion
- 1/2 cup dried cranberries
- 1/4 cup fresh parsley, chopped
- 2 tbsp olive oil
- 1 tsp dried thyme
- Salt and pepper to taste

Substitutions

None

Directions

1. Preheat oven to 375°F (190°C).
2. Brush the cut sides of the acorn squash halves with olive oil and sprinkle with dried thyme, salt, and pepper.
3. Place the squash halves cut-side down on a baking sheet and roast for 30-35 minutes until tender.
4. While the squash is roasting, heat olive oil in a skillet and sauté diced butternut squash, red bell pepper, and red onion until softened.
5. Stir in cooked quinoa, dried cranberries, and fresh parsley. Season with salt and pepper.
6. Once the squash is roasted, flip the halves and stuff them with the quinoa mixture.
7. Return to the oven for an additional 10 minutes until everything is heated through.
8. Serve your quinoa-stuffed acorn squash as a wholesome and visually appealing dinner.
9. Enjoy the flavors and textures of this dish.

4
servings

380
calories

30
minutes

Vegan BBQ Black Bean Bowl

A satisfying bowl with BBQ-spiced black beans, roasted veggies, and quinoa.

Ingredients:

- 2 cups cooked quinoa
- 2 cans black beans, drained and rinsed
- 2 cups mixed bell peppers, sliced
- 1 red onion, sliced
- 1 cup corn kernels (fresh or frozen)
- 1/2 cup BBQ sauce
- 1/4 cup fresh cilantro, chopped
- 1 lime, cut into wedges
- Salt and pepper to taste

Directions

1. Preheat oven to 425°F (220°C).
2. Toss sliced bell peppers and red onion with olive oil, salt, and pepper.
3. Roast in the oven for 20-25 minutes until slightly charred.
4. In a skillet, heat black beans with BBQ sauce over medium heat until heated through.
5. Serve cooked quinoa in bowls, top with BBQ black beans, roasted veggies, and corn kernels.
6. Garnish with fresh cilantro and lime wedges.
7. Enjoy your BBQ black bean bowl as a hearty and flavor-packed dinner.

Substitutions

None

4
servings

150
calories

30
minutes

Vegan Lemon Garlic Roasted Brussels Sprouts

Ingredients:

- 1 lb Brussels sprouts, trimmed and halved
- 2 cloves garlic, minced
- Juice and zest of 1 lemon
- 2 tbsp olive oil
- Salt and pepper to taste

Substitutions

None

A simple yet delicious side dish featuring roasted Brussels sprouts with a zesty lemon garlic glaze.

Directions

1. Preheat oven to 400°F (200°C).
2. In a bowl, toss halved Brussels sprouts with olive oil, minced garlic, lemon zest, lemon juice, salt, and pepper.
3. Spread Brussels sprouts in a single layer on a baking sheet.
4. Roast for 20-25 minutes, tossing halfway through, until they are tender and slightly crispy.
5. Serve your lemon garlic roasted Brussels sprouts as a delightful and tangy side dish.
6. Enjoy the vibrant flavors of this simple yet delicious recipe.

4
servings

320
calories

45
minutes

Vegan Lentil Shepherd's Pie

A vegan twist on the classic shepherd's pie, loaded with hearty lentils and topped with mashed potatoes.

Ingredients:

- 4 cups mashed potatoes (prepared)
- 2 cups cooked green or brown lentils
- 1 onion, chopped
- 2 carrots, diced
- 2 cloves garlic, minced
- 1 cup frozen peas
- 1 cup vegetable broth
- 1 tbsp tomato paste
- 1 tsp dried thyme
- Salt and pepper to taste

Directions

1. Preheat oven to 375°F (190°C).
2. In a skillet, sauté chopped onions, diced carrots, and minced garlic until softened.
3. Stir in cooked lentils, frozen peas, vegetable broth, tomato paste, dried thyme, salt, and pepper.
4. Simmer for 10-15 minutes until the mixture thickens.
5. Transfer the lentil mixture to a baking dish.
6. Spread mashed potatoes evenly over the lentil mixture.
7. Bake for 20-25 minutes until the top is golden and the filling is bubbling.
8. Serve your lentil shepherd's pie as a hearty and comforting dinner.
9. Enjoy this vegan twist on a classic comfort food.

Substitutions

None

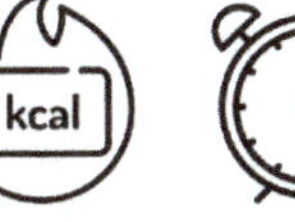

4
servings

320
calories

30
minutes

Vegan Soba Noodle Stir-Fry

A quick and flavorful stir-fry with soba noodles, tofu, and an array of colorful vegetables.

Ingredients:

- 8 oz soba noodles
- 1 block firm tofu, cubed
- 2 cups broccoli florets
- 1 red bell pepper, thinly sliced
- 1 carrot, julienned
- 1/2 cup snow peas, trimmed
- 1/4 cup soy sauce (or tamari for gluten-free)
- 2 tbsp maple syrup
- 1 tbsp rice vinegar
- 2 cloves garlic, minced
- 1 tsp grated ginger
- 1 tbsp sesame oil
- Sesame seeds and chopped green onions for garnish

Substitutions

Tamari can be used for a gluten-free version.

Directions

1. Cook soba noodles according to package instructions until al dente.
2. In a large skillet, stir-fry cubed tofu until browned and crispy.
3. Remove tofu from the skillet and set aside.
4. In the same skillet, stir-fry broccoli florets, red bell pepper, julienned carrot, and snow peas until tender-crisp.
5. In a bowl, whisk together soy sauce, maple syrup, rice vinegar, minced garlic, grated ginger, and sesame oil.
6. Return tofu to the skillet and pour the sauce over the tofu and vegetables.
7. Add cooked soba noodles and toss to coat everything in the sauce.
8. Serve your soba noodle stir-fry garnished with sesame seeds and chopped green onions.
9. Enjoy this quick and vibrant stir-fry.

4
servings

280
calories

50
minutes

Vegan Eggplant and Zucchini Lasagna

A hearty and layered lasagna with tender eggplant, zucchini, and a flavorful tomato sauce.

Ingredients:

- 1 large eggplant, thinly sliced lengthwise
- 2 large zucchini, thinly sliced lengthwise
- 2 cups marinara sauce (store-bought or homemade)
- 1 cup vegan ricotta cheese
- 1 cup vegan mozzarella cheese, shredded
- 1/4 cup fresh basil leaves
- 2 cloves garlic, minced
- 1 tsp dried oregano
- Salt and pepper to taste

Substitutions

None

Directions

1. Preheat oven to 375°F (190°C).
2. In a bowl, combine vegan ricotta cheese, minced garlic, dried oregano, salt, and pepper.
3. In a baking dish, layer eggplant slices, zucchini slices, marinara sauce, and vegan ricotta mixture.
4. Repeat the layers until all ingredients are used, finishing with a layer of vegan mozzarella cheese.
5. Cover with foil and bake for 30 minutes.
6. Remove the foil and bake for an additional 15-20 minutes until the lasagna is bubbly and the cheese is melted and slightly golden.
7. Garnish with fresh basil leaves.
8. Serve your eggplant and zucchini lasagna as a satisfying and comforting dinner.
9. Enjoy the layers of flavor in this vegan twist on a classic dish.

4
servings

180
calories

25
minutes

Vegan Creamy Tomato and Basil Soup

Ingredients:

- 2 cans diced tomatoes
- 1 onion, chopped
- 2 cloves garlic, minced
- 1 cup vegetable broth
- 1/2 cup unsweetened almond milk
- 1/4 cup fresh basil leaves, chopped
- 2 tbsp olive oil
- Salt and pepper to taste

Substitutions

None

A velvety tomato soup with a touch of basil, perfect for a cozy evening meal.

Directions

1. In a pot, sauté chopped onions and minced garlic in olive oil until translucent.
2. Add canned diced tomatoes (with juice) and vegetable broth.
3. Simmer for about 15 minutes.
4. Use an immersion blender to puree the soup until smooth.
5. Stir in unsweetened almond milk and chopped fresh basil.
6. Simmer for an additional 5 minutes to heat through.
7. Season with salt and pepper.
8. Serve your creamy tomato and basil soup as a comforting and velvety dinner.
9. Enjoy the classic flavors of this heartwarming soup.

4
servings

320
calories

45
minutes

Vegan Moroccan Stuffed Bell Peppers

Bell peppers stuffed with a flavorful mixture of quinoa, chickpeas, and Moroccan spices.

Ingredients:

- 4 large bell peppers, tops removed and seeds removed
- 1 cup cooked quinoa
- 1 can chickpeas, drained and rinsed
- 1/2 cup diced tomatoes (canned or fresh)
- 1/4 cup raisins
- 1/4 cup fresh cilantro, chopped
- 2 cloves garlic, minced
- 1 tsp ground cumin
- 1/2 tsp ground coriander
- Salt and pepper to taste

Directions

1. Preheat oven to 375°F (190°C).
2. In a bowl, combine cooked quinoa, chickpeas, diced tomatoes, raisins, chopped fresh cilantro, minced garlic, ground cumin, ground coriander, salt, and pepper.
3. Stuff the mixture into the hollowed bell peppers.
4. Place stuffed peppers in a baking dish and cover with foil.
5. Bake for 30 minutes.
6. Remove the foil and bake for an additional 15 minutes until peppers are tender.
7. Serve your Moroccan stuffed peppers as a flavorful and satisfying dinner.
8. Enjoy the exotic blend of spices in every bite.

Substitutions

None

Chapter 10
Superfood Breakfasts to Start the Day Right

2
servings

180
calories

10
minutes

Vegan Dragon Fruit Smoothie

Ingredients:

- 1 dragon fruit, scooped out
- 1 banana, peeled
- 1 cup coconut water
- Juice of 1 lime
- 1 tbsp honey or maple syrup (optional)
- Ice cubes
- Fresh mint leaves for garnish

A vibrant and refreshing smoothie featuring dragon fruit, a tropical superfood.

Directions

1. Place dragon fruit, banana, coconut water, lime juice, honey (if using), and ice cubes in a blender.
2. Blend until smooth and creamy.
3. Pour into glasses and garnish with fresh mint leaves.
4. Serve your dragon fruit smoothie as a vibrant and refreshing breakfast.
5. Enjoy the tropical flavors and the burst of color.

Substitutions

Use agave nectar for a vegan sweetener.

2
servings

300
calories

15
minutes

Vegan Acai Bowl with Superfood Toppings

An acai bowl topped with a medley of superfoods like granola, berries, and chia seeds.

Ingredients:

- 2 packets frozen acai puree
- 1 banana, frozen
- 1/2 cup almond milk (or any plant-based milk)
- 1 cup mixed berries
- 1/4 cup granola
- 1 tbsp chia seeds
- Fresh berries and sliced banana for topping
- Drizzle of honey or maple syrup (optional)

Directions

1. Run the frozen acai puree packets under warm water to slightly thaw.
2. In a blender, combine thawed acai, frozen banana, and almond milk.
3. Blend until smooth and thick.
4. Pour the acai mixture into bowls.
5. Top with mixed berries, granola, chia seeds, fresh berries, sliced banana, and a drizzle of honey or maple syrup (if desired).
6. Serve your acai bowl with superfood toppings as a nutritious and colorful breakfast.
7. Enjoy the burst of flavors and textures.

Substitutions

Use agave nectar for a vegan sweetener.

2
servings

220
calories

5
minutes

Vegan Spirulina Chia Pudding

Ingredients:

- 1/4 cup chia seeds
- 1 cup almond milk (or any plant-based milk)
- 1 tsp spirulina powder
- 1 tsp maple syrup (or more to taste)
- Fresh berries for garnish

Substitutions

None

A vibrant green chia pudding infused with the superfood spirulina.

Directions

1. In a jar or bowl, combine chia seeds, almond milk, spirulina powder, and maple syrup.
2. Stir well to mix all ingredients thoroughly.
3. Cover and refrigerate for at least 2 hours or overnight, allowing the chia seeds to absorb the liquid and thicken.
4. Before serving, give the pudding a good stir.
5. Garnish with fresh berries.
6. Serve your spirulina chia pudding as a vibrant and nutritious breakfast.
7. Enjoy the health benefits of spirulina in this delightful pudding.

2
servings

240
calories

10
minutes

Vegan Turmeric and Cinnamon Oatmeal

Creamy oatmeal infused with the anti-inflammatory superfoods turmeric and cinnamon.

Ingredients:

- 1 cup rolled oats
- 2 cups almond milk (or any plant-based milk)
- 1 tsp ground turmeric
- 1/2 tsp ground cinnamon
- 1 tsp maple syrup (or more to taste)
- Sliced banana and chopped nuts for topping

Directions

1. In a saucepan, combine rolled oats, almond milk, ground turmeric, and ground cinnamon.
2. Cook over medium heat, stirring frequently, until the oats are tender and the mixture thickens, about 5-7 minutes.
3. Stir in maple syrup to sweeten, adjusting to your taste.
4. Serve your turmeric and cinnamon oatmeal in bowls, topped with sliced banana and chopped nuts.
5. Enjoy this creamy and spiced breakfast that's both comforting and nutritious.

Substitutions

Use agave nectar for a vegan sweetener.

2 servings

350 calories

15 minutes

A hearty breakfast burrito filled with superfoods like quinoa, avocado, and kale.

Vegan Superfood Breakfast Burrito

Ingredients:

- 2 large whole wheat tortillas
- 1 cup cooked quinoa
- 1 cup kale, stems removed and chopped
- 1 avocado, sliced
- 1/2 cup black beans, drained and rinsed
- 1/4 cup salsa
- 1/4 cup vegan cheese (optional)
- Salt and pepper to taste

Directions

1. In a skillet, sauté chopped kale until wilted.
2. Warm whole wheat tortillas in a dry skillet or microwave.
3. Lay out each tortilla and assemble with cooked quinoa, sautéed kale, sliced avocado, black beans, salsa, and vegan cheese (if using).
4. Season with salt and pepper.
5. Fold in the sides and roll up the tortilla to create a burrito.
6. Serve your superfood breakfast burrito as a hearty and nutritious morning meal.
7. Enjoy the flavors and textures of this satisfying breakfast.

Substitutions

None

 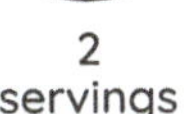  

2 servings

280 calories

20 minutes

Vegan Blueberry Protein Pancakes

Ingredients:

- 1 cup whole wheat flour
- 1 scoop vegan protein powder (vanilla or berry flavor)
- 1 tbsp baking powder
- 1/2 tsp cinnamon
- 1 cup almond milk (or any plant-based milk)
- 1/2 cup blueberries (fresh or frozen)
- 1 tsp vanilla extract
- Maple syrup for drizzling

Substitutions

None

Fluffy blueberry pancakes packed with plant-based protein for a powerful breakfast.

Directions

1. In a bowl, whisk together whole wheat flour, vegan protein powder, baking powder, and cinnamon.
2. Add almond milk and vanilla extract, stirring until the batter is smooth.
3. Gently fold in blueberries.
4. Heat a non-stick skillet or griddle over medium heat and lightly grease with oil or cooking spray.
5. Pour 1/4 cup portions of batter onto the skillet to make pancakes.
6. Cook until bubbles form on the surface, then flip and cook until golden brown on both sides.
7. Serve your blueberry protein pancakes with a drizzle of maple syrup.
8. Enjoy these fluffy and protein-packed pancakes for a powerful breakfast.

2
servings

230
calories

10
minutes

Vegan Coconut and Maca Smoothie

Ingredients:

- 1 cup coconut milk (canned or carton)
- 1 banana, peeled
- 2 tbsp maca powder
- 1 tbsp almond butter
- 1 tbsp shredded coconut
- 1 tsp maple syrup (or more to taste)
- Ice cubes

Substitutions

None

A creamy and energizing smoothie featuring the superfood maca and the tropical taste of coconut.

Directions

1. Place coconut milk, banana, maca powder, almond butter, shredded coconut, maple syrup (if using), and ice cubes in a blender.
2. Blend until smooth and creamy.
3. Pour into glasses.
4. Serve your coconut and maca smoothie as a creamy and energizing breakfast.
5. Enjoy the unique flavor combination of coconut and maca.

2
servings

40
calories

10
minutes

Vegan Chaga Mushroom Latte

Ingredients:

- 2 cups almond milk (or any plant-based milk)
- 2 tsp chaga mushroom powder
- 2 tsp maple syrup (or more to taste)
- A pinch of ground cinnamon (optional)

Substitutions

None

Easy

A cozy latte infused with chaga mushrooms, known for their potential health benefits.

Directions

1. In a saucepan, heat almond milk over medium heat until hot but not boiling.
2. Whisk in chaga mushroom powder and maple syrup (adjust to your taste).
3. Add a pinch of ground cinnamon if desired.
4. Whisk until well combined and frothy.
5. Pour your chaga mushroom latte into mugs.
6. Serve as a cozy and potentially beneficial morning beverage.
7. Enjoy the earthy flavors and potential health perks of chaga mushrooms.

 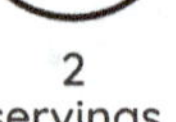  

2
servings

260
calories

10
minutes

Vegan Green Tea Chia Parfait

Ingredients:

- 1/4 cup chia seeds
- 1 cup almond milk (or any plant-based milk)
- 2 tsp matcha green tea powder
- 1 tsp maple syrup (or more to taste)
- 1/2 cup granola
- Sliced kiwi and strawberries for topping

Substitutions

None

A layered parfait with green tea chia pudding, granola, and fresh fruit for a refreshing breakfast.

Directions

1. In a jar or bowl, combine chia seeds, almond milk, matcha green tea powder, and maple syrup.
2. Stir well to mix all ingredients thoroughly.
3. Cover and refrigerate for at least 2 hours or overnight, allowing the chia seeds to absorb the liquid and thicken.
4. Before serving, give the green tea chia pudding a good stir.
5. Layer the parfait with green tea chia pudding, granola, and fresh fruit.
6. Serve your green tea chia parfait as a refreshing and energizing breakfast.
7. Enjoy the balance of flavors and textures.

2
servings

320
calories

20
minutes

Vegan Pomegranate Quinoa Breakfast Bowl

Ingredients:

- 1 cup cooked quinoa
- 1/2 cup pomegranate seeds
- 1/4 cup chopped almonds
- 1/4 cup coconut yogurt
- 2 tbsp maple syrup (or more to taste)

A nutrient-packed breakfast bowl with quinoa, pomegranate seeds, and a drizzle of maple syrup.

Directions

1. In bowls, divide cooked quinoa.
2. Top with pomegranate seeds and chopped almonds.
3. Drizzle with coconut yogurt and maple syrup (adjust to your taste).
4. Serve your pomegranate quinoa breakfast bowl as a nutrient-packed morning delight.
5. Enjoy the vibrant colors and flavors.

Substitutions

None

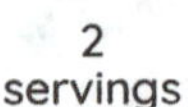

2 servings

200 calories

10 minutes

Vegan Goji Berry and Chia Smoothie

Ingredients:

- 1 cup almond milk (or any plant-based milk)
- 2 tbsp goji berries
- 1 tbsp chia seeds
- 1 banana, peeled
- 1/2 cup frozen mixed berries
- 1 tsp agave nectar (or more to taste)
- Ice cubes

Substitutions

Use maple syrup for a different sweetener.

A nourishing smoothie featuring goji berries and chia seeds for a burst of antioxidants.

Directions

1. Place almond milk, goji berries, chia seeds, banana, frozen mixed berries, and agave nectar (adjust to your taste) in a blender.
2. Blend until smooth and creamy.
3. Add ice cubes and blend again until well combined.
4. Pour into glasses.
5. Serve your goji berry and chia smoothie as a nourishing and antioxidant-rich breakfast.
6. Enjoy the burst of antioxidants and natural sweetness.

Chapter 11
Superfood Brunch Delights

2
servings

220
calories

20
minutes

Vegan Spirulina Pancakes

Ingredients:

- 1 cup whole wheat flour
- 2 tbsp spirulina powder
- 2 tbsp coconut sugar (or any sweetener of choice)
- 1 tsp baking powder
- 1 cup almond milk (or any plant-based milk)
- 1 tsp vanilla extract
- 1 tbsp apple cider vinegar
- 1/2 cup fresh blueberries (optional)
- Coconut oil for greasing

Substitutions

None

Green and fluffy pancakes infused with spirulina, a superfood known for its vibrant color and nutrients.

Directions

1. In a bowl, whisk together whole wheat flour, spirulina powder, coconut sugar, and baking powder.
2. In a separate bowl, combine almond milk, vanilla extract, and apple cider vinegar. Let it sit for a few minutes to curdle.
3. Pour the wet mixture into the dry mixture and stir until well combined.
4. Fold in fresh blueberries if desired.
5. Heat a non-stick skillet or griddle over medium heat and lightly grease with coconut oil.
6. Pour 1/4 cup portions of batter onto the skillet to make pancakes.
7. Cook until bubbles form on the surface, then flip and cook until golden brown on both sides.
8. Serve your spirulina pancakes as a green and nutritious brunch.
9. Enjoy the unique color and flavor of these superfood pancakes.

2
servings

280
calories

25
minutes

Vegan Sweet Potato Breakfast Hash

Ingredients:

- 2 cups sweet potatoes, diced
- 1/2 onion, chopped
- 1 bell pepper, diced
- 1 cup spinach leaves
- 1/2 cup black beans, drained and rinsed
- 1 tsp paprika
- 1/2 tsp cumin
- Salt and pepper to taste
- Olive oil for cooking

Substitutions

None

A savory and hearty hash featuring sweet potatoes and a medley of veggies, perfect for brunch.

Directions

1. In a skillet, heat olive oil over medium heat.
2. Add chopped onions and diced sweet potatoes.
3. Sauté until sweet potatoes are tender and slightly crispy, about 15-20 minutes.
4. Stir in diced bell pepper, black beans, paprika, cumin, salt, and pepper.
5. Cook for an additional 5 minutes until the bell pepper is tender.
6. Add spinach leaves and cook until wilted.
7. Serve your sweet potato breakfast hash as a savory and satisfying brunch.
8. Enjoy the flavors and textures of this hearty dish.

2
servings

220
calories

5
minutes

Vegan Matcha Chia Pudding

Ingredients:

- 1/4 cup chia seeds
- 1 cup almond milk (or any plant-based milk)
- 2 tsp matcha green tea powder
- 2 tsp maple syrup (or more to taste)
- Fresh berries for garnish

Substitutions

None

A vibrant green chia pudding infused with the antioxidant-rich superfood matcha.

Directions

1. In a jar or bowl, combine chia seeds, almond milk, matcha green tea powder, and maple syrup.
2. Stir well to mix all ingredients thoroughly.
3. Cover and refrigerate for at least 2 hours or overnight, allowing the chia seeds to absorb the liquid and thicken.
4. Before serving, give the matcha chia pudding a good stir.
5. Garnish with fresh berries.
6. Serve your matcha chia pudding as a vibrant and antioxidant-rich brunch.
7. Enjoy the health benefits and beautiful green hue.

2 servings

320 calories

15 minutes

Vegan Quinoa and Kale Breakfast Salad

A refreshing breakfast salad with quinoa, kale, and a zesty lemon vinaigrette.

Ingredients:

- 1 cup cooked quinoa
- 2 cups kale, stems removed and chopped
- 1/2 cup cherry tomatoes, halved
- 1/4 cup cucumber, diced
- 1/4 cup red onion, thinly sliced
- 1/4 cup fresh parsley, chopped
- Juice of 1 lemon
- 2 tbsp olive oil
- Salt and pepper to taste
- Toasted pumpkin seeds for garnish

Directions

1. In a large bowl, combine cooked quinoa, chopped kale, cherry tomatoes, diced cucumber, sliced red onion, and fresh parsley.
2. In a small bowl, whisk together lemon juice, olive oil, salt, and pepper to make the vinaigrette.
3. Drizzle the lemon vinaigrette over the salad and toss to coat all ingredients.
4. Garnish with toasted pumpkin seeds.
5. Serve your quinoa and kale breakfast salad as a refreshing and nutritious brunch.
6. Enjoy the zesty flavors and crunch of this salad.

Substitutions

None

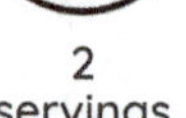

2
servings

240
calories

10
minutes

Vegan Turmeric Ginger Smoothie Bowl

Ingredients:

- 2 frozen bananas
- 1 tsp ground turmeric
- 1 tsp fresh ginger, grated
- 1 cup almond milk (or any plant-based milk)
- Toppings: sliced kiwi, shredded coconut, chia seeds

Substitutions

None

A vibrant smoothie bowl with the anti-inflammatory power of turmeric and the zing of ginger.

Directions

1. In a blender, combine frozen bananas, ground turmeric, grated fresh ginger, and almond milk.
2. Blend until smooth and creamy.
3. Pour the turmeric ginger smoothie into bowls.
4. Top with sliced kiwi, shredded coconut, and chia seeds.
5. Serve your turmeric ginger smoothie bowl as a vibrant and anti-inflammatory brunch.
6. Enjoy the flavors and health benefits of this bowl.

2 servings

320 calories

25 minutes

Vegan Blueberry and Acai Protein Waffles

Protein-packed waffles with the antioxidant goodness of acai and the sweetness of blueberries.

Ingredients:

- 1 cup whole wheat flour
- 1 scoop vegan protein powder (vanilla or berry flavor)
- 1 tbsp acai berry powder
- 1 tbsp baking powder
- 1/2 cup almond milk (or any plant-based milk)
- 1/2 cup fresh blueberries
- 1 tsp vanilla extract
- Maple syrup for drizzling

Substitutions

None

Directions

1. In a bowl, whisk together whole wheat flour, vegan protein powder, acai berry powder, and baking powder.
2. Add almond milk and vanilla extract, stirring until the batter is smooth.
3. Gently fold in fresh blueberries.
4. Preheat your waffle iron and lightly grease it.
5. Pour the batter onto the waffle iron and cook according to the manufacturer's instructions until waffles are golden brown and crisp.
6. Serve your blueberry and acai protein waffles with a drizzle of maple syrup.
7. Enjoy these protein-packed waffles for a satisfying brunch.
8. Experience the antioxidant-rich flavors.

2
servings

280
calories

15
minutes

Vegan Avocado and Spinach Breakfast Wrap

Ingredients:

- 2 large whole wheat tortillas
- 1 avocado, sliced
- 2 cups fresh spinach leaves
- 1/2 cup cherry tomatoes, halved
- 1/4 cup red onion, thinly sliced
- Hot sauce or salsa for drizzling (optional)
- Salt and pepper to taste

Substitutions

None

A flavorful breakfast wrap with creamy avocado, fresh spinach, and a touch of spice.

Directions

1. Warm whole wheat tortillas in a dry skillet or microwave.
2. Lay out each tortilla and assemble with sliced avocado, fresh spinach leaves, cherry tomatoes, and red onion.
3. Add a drizzle of hot sauce or salsa if you like some spice.
4. Season with salt and pepper.
5. Fold in the sides and roll up the tortilla to create a wrap.
6. Serve your avocado and spinach breakfast wrap as a flavorful and satisfying brunch.
7. Enjoy the creamy, crunchy, and spicy combination.

2
servings

260
calories

10
minutes

Vegan Chocolate Raspberry Chia Parfait

Ingredients:

- 1/4 cup chia seeds
- 1 cup almond milk (or any plant-based milk)
- 2 tbsp cocoa powder
- 2 tbsp maple syrup (or more to taste)
- 1 cup fresh raspberries
- Vegan chocolate chips for garnish (optional)

Substitutions

None

A decadent chocolate chia parfait with layers of raspberry compote for a brunch treat.

Directions

1. In a jar or bowl, combine chia seeds, almond milk, cocoa powder, and maple syrup.
2. Stir well to mix all ingredients thoroughly.
3. Cover and refrigerate for at least 2 hours or overnight, allowing the chia seeds to absorb the liquid and thicken.
4. Before serving, give the chocolate chia pudding a good stir.
5. In serving glasses or bowls, layer the chocolate chia pudding with fresh raspberries.
6. Garnish with vegan chocolate chips if desired.
7. Serve your chocolate raspberry chia parfait as a decadent and indulgent brunch treat.
8. Enjoy the rich chocolate and fruity flavors.

2 servings · **340 calories** · **20 minutes**

Vegan Superfood Breakfast Tacos

Ingredients:

- 4 small whole wheat tortillas
- 1 cup cooked quinoa
- 1 avocado, sliced
- 1/2 cup black beans, drained and rinsed
- 1/4 cup salsa
- 1/4 cup fresh cilantro, chopped
- Juice of 1 lime
- Salt and pepper to taste

Substitutions

None

Flavorful breakfast tacos filled with superfoods like quinoa, avocado, and salsa.

Directions

1. Warm whole wheat tortillas in a dry skillet or microwave.
2. Lay out each tortilla and assemble with cooked quinoa, sliced avocado, black beans, salsa, fresh cilantro, and a squeeze of lime juice.
3. Season with salt and pepper.
4. Fold in the sides and roll up the tortilla to create tacos.
5. Serve your superfood breakfast tacos as a flavorful and nutritious brunch.
6. Enjoy the combination of textures and zesty flavors.

We have a small favor to ask

As we delve deeper into the realm of "Vegan Superfood," exploring the nourishing and vibrant world of plant-based superfoods, I want to take a moment to express my heartfelt gratitude to all of you, the intrepid seekers of healthier and more wholesome eating. Together, we've embarked on a journey to discover the delicious and transformative power of plant-based superfoods.

Now, in the midst of this culinary adventure, I have a humble request. In the world of small publishers like us, reviews are akin to the nutrients that sustain our culinary creations – they are the vital essence that keeps our passion alive and thriving.

If you've found inspiration in our collection of plant-based superfood recipes, if you've marveled at the incredible flavors and health benefits these ingredients bring to your table, I kindly ask for your support. Please take a moment to revisit the app or website where you acquired this book, where you'll discover that cherished review button. There, you can bestow upon us a rating and share a brief sentence or two about your experience.

Your review isn't just feedback; it's a connection, a beacon that guides fellow health-conscious food enthusiasts to these pages. It strengthens our mission to make plant-based superfood dining accessible and mouthwateringly delightful. Every review you leave is like a sprinkle of chia seeds, adding nourishment to our passion for this culinary journey. Rest assured, we read each one with genuine appreciation and anticipation.

And if, by any chance, you've noticed a minor hiccup or oversight along the way, please understand that we've poured our heart and soul into crafting this superfood adventure. We've aimed for perfection, but even the most meticulous chefs can sometimes overlook a detail in the hustle and bustle of the kitchen. Your understanding is the gentle reminder to savor the journey rather than obsess over the destination.

So, as we return to the recipes, invigorated by the energy of plant-based superfoods, let's continue to savor the art of nourishing and flavorful eating. Until our paths cross again amidst the vibrant colors of fresh produce and the zest of superfood smoothies, stay curious, keep experimenting, and revel in the joy of every superfood-infused bite. Your culinary journey continues, and we're profoundly grateful to have been a part of it.